COPENHAGEN
TRAVEL
GUIDE

Captivating Adventures Through Nordic Beauty,

Historic Waterfronts, Danish Landmarks, Hidden Gems, and More

Welcome Aboard, Discover
Your Limited-Time Free Bonus!

Hello, traveler! Welcome to the Captivating Travels family, and thanks for grabbing a copy of this book! Since you've chosen to join us on this journey, we'd like to offer you something special.

Check out the link below for a FREE Ultimate Travel Checklist eBook & Printable PDF to make your travel planning stress-free and enjoyable.

But that's not all - you'll also gain access to our exclusive email list with even more free e-books and insider travel tips. Well, what are you waiting for? Click the link below to join and embark on your next adventure with ease.

Access your bonus here: https://livetolearn.lpages.co/ checklist/

Or, Scan the QR code!

TABLE OF CONTENTS

INTRODUCTION

This guide to Copenhagen aims to provide the most up-to-date information about the city and some lesser-known insider secrets about real gems worth visiting. The book is compiled so that you get to see the best of every part of Copenhagen with tips on making the most of your time and having the best experience. Are you ready to get started on your Copenhagen journey? There is no better place to start than this comprehensive guide, ideal for first-time visitors.

Copenhagen, the capital of Denmark, is situated on the islands of Zealand and Amager, in the East of Denmark. What was once a small Viking settlement and fishing village is today one of the busiest, biggest, and most spectacular cities in Europe, if not the entire world.

Here, you can walk among picturesque streets, walkways, and waterfronts. The lively cafes flavor the air with the scent of delicious Danish pastries, the calm waters lap against docked fishing boats waiting to go out for their next catch, and the cobblestone streets tell a tale of a fascinating past. It's a fusion of historic, exquisitely preserved architecture, trendy modern neighborhoods, and bustling commercial areas, all neatly packed into a clean and natural environment divided by waterways throughout the city toward the open expanse of the Oresund.

Copenhagen is home to nearly 1.4 million people and is spread across ten zones or districts.

Indre By, which translates to *Inner City*, is Copenhagen's central (and oldest) part. This historic area is home to the most iconic landmarks in the entire region, filled with museums and galleries that are significant in keeping the past alive.

Close by is Frederiksberg, an upscale urban area known for elegant architecture, lush green streets, modern construction, and the Frederiksberg Gardens. Adjacent to Frederiksberg, you will find Vesterbro, another modern area in Copenhagen with lively nightlife, contemporary entertainment, and high-end shopping options. You will find plenty of bars and restaurants with a modern vibe here.

Another interesting place to see is Osterbro. It is primarily a residential area filled with green spaces, such as Faelledparken and Soerne, but its cozy environment makes it a popular tourist attraction. It has plenty of modern amenities, like cafes and eateries, where you can spend a relaxing afternoon or evening.

Within Osterbro, you will find Nordre Frihavn, which is popular for its waterfront locations, marinas, and modern developments.

Another particularly popular spot is Norrebro. This area is known for its diverse, multicultural environment, relaxed atmosphere, outstanding food scene, and indie shops. It is home to the Assistens Cemetery. Not far away is Bispebjerg, a large residential area home to one of the largest hospitals in the area (Bispebjerg Hospital).

Just off the shore of Copenhagen, you will find Amager, an island divided into Amager East and Amager West, connected to Copenhagen by bridges and a metro tunnel. Amager East is well-known for its beach (Amager Strandpark) and residential developments. On the West Amager are industrial zones, offices, the DR Byen Complex, and a few residential areas.

Bronshoj-Husum is a suburban area with a nice mix of residential areas, parks, and various amenities. Close to Bronshoj-Husum is Vanlose, a large residential area that offers green spaces, shops, and commercial activity.

Overall, Copenhagen is a unique experience. It is ultra-modern yet still in tune with its roots. When new developments are created, the natural elements are undisturbed.

Let the adventure begin!

1

GET TO KNOW COPENHAGEN

WHERE IS COPENHAGEN?

The Kingdom of Denmark, which includes Greenland, sits in 12th place on the list of the largest countries in the world according to land mass, with a size of over 2 million square kilometers. Denmark consists of over 1400 islands, of which just 443 have been named. Of the named islands, approximately 78 are inhabited, while the bulk of the population resides on the islands of North Jutland Island, Funen, and Zealand.

Copenhagen, on the eastern coast of Zealand, is near neighboring Sweden. Moreover, it is a geographically strategic location as it connects Denmark with Northern Europe through the Baltic Sea. Historically, this has proven to be a valuable asset and has played a significant role in Denmark's economic, political, and even cultural evolution.

HISTORY

Copenhagen's roots can be traced back to the eleventh century when Vikings settled to establish a fishing village and a small trading settlement to accommodate their otherwise nomadic population. Being on the narrow strait between Zealand and Scania made it an ideal location for maritime activities and commerce.

By the 12th century, Copenhagen had slowly but surely become well-known as a prominent commerce center. Bishop Absalon's construction of the Absalon castle in the early 12th century further strengthened Copenhagen's status.

The exterior of the Absalon Castle.¹

During the medieval period, Copenhagen's location made it ideal for trade and commerce in the Baltic Sea region. It was influenced by the Hanseatic League during this time, which was a powerful trading alliance operating in Northern Europe.

Later, during the reign of King Christian IV (1588-1648), significant developments were made to the city's architecture and infrastructure. Major landmarks, such as the Rosenborg Castle, Rundetaarn Tower, and the Borsen Stock Exchange, were built.

With all this development, the city became a major commercial player during the 18th and 19th centuries, and Nyhavn (New Harbor) became a central trading point. The Danish Navy played a significant role in providing security and maintaining maritime connections across the Baltic Sea and beyond.

In the late 19th and early 20th centuries, Copenhagen experienced industrial growth. Projects such as the Copenhagen Central Station (1847) played a pivotal role in providing essential facilities, further cementing the city's growth and appeal as a commercial hub.

COPENHAGEN'S ROLE IN THE FORMATION OF DENMARK

Copenhagen played two roles that were integral to the formation of Denmark. One was the economic stability it provided as a major center for trade and commerce. The other was its defense by developing fortifications, such as Kastellet, that secured the city and the country. The 1801 Battle of Copenhagen is a prime example of how the well-equipped Danish navy and Copenhagen's strategic location made it an excellent defensive resource.

As Denmark shifted from an absolute monarchy to a constitutional monarchy in 1849, there was a political and constitutional element. The Danish constitution establishing the monarchy and parliamentary system was signed in Copenhagen, taking Danish governance to new heights.

Lastly, during World War II, the Danish resistance movement fighting against Nazi occupation was primarily based in Copenhagen, adding to the city's influence on the nation. Naturally, there was immense destruction in Copenhagen after the Second World War, and the government went to great lengths to restore the city and re-build it bigger and stronger. Moreover, the city hosted multiple international events that brought more attention to not only Copenhagen but also Denmark, which helped the country recover from the crisis of the World War and start a new journey of growth.

COPENHAGEN VS. OTHER NORDIC COUNTRIES

Copenhagen benefits from its geographic position in the region. It has excellent access to Northern Europe and Scandinavian countries, particularly Sweden and Norway. Its proximity to Northern Europe, facilitated by the Oresund Bridge, makes it a major transport link, and Kastrup Airport is an essential air-travel gateway for the entire region. Copenhagen has access to waterways and plenty of maritime history, making it a significant player in European trade and shipping networks.

Oresund Bridge.[2]

Due to its strategic location, it has been a hotspot for people from all over Europe and Scandinavia. Today, Copenhagen is a cosmopolitan city with a diverse population that reflects its influence from all parts of the region.

Copenhagen is an economic powerhouse with numerous multinational companies headquartered in Copenhagen, including tech companies, financial giants, and other institutions.

The city is a serious player in the region's politics. It is one of the chief influencers in EU affairs and has a powerful standing in political and diplomatic matters. Copenhagen is often the preferred venue for conferences, summits, cultural events, and other activities that facilitate dialogue and cooperation locally and internationally.

A BIT ABOUT COPENHAGENERS

One of the highlights of Copenhageners is the *hygge* lifestyle (pronounced Hoo-Guh). This lifestyle embraces comfort, warmth, togetherness, and appreciation of the simpler things in life and is central to life in Copenhagen.

Copenhagen is all about enjoying cozy moments. They strive to make comfort, togetherness, relaxation, and a tight-knit social life an essential part of their day-to-day life. Even architecture in Copenhagen focuses on soft lighting, comfortable furnishings, cozy home layout plans, and personal touches throughout their spaces to promote well-being and happiness.

The small things in life bring Copenhagen the most joy. You will often see locals sitting on a park bench soaking in the sunlight, enjoying a hot cup of coffee or tea while they read a book, enjoying other hobbies like crafting and listening to music, or just enjoying a delicious Danish pastry.

Copenhageners are highly focused on sustainable and eco-friendly living practices. The city promotes cycling as the primary form of transport. There are bike lanes on every road in the city, several bike-sharing programs, and basic cultural values about biking for transport, leisure, and exercise. The city invests heavily in reducing carbon emissions and creating green spaces and has developed numerous green areas for residents to enjoy biodiversity.

OVERVIEW OF COPENHAGEN

One of the highlights of Copenhagen is the incredibly delicious traditional Danish cuisine – Smorrebrod (smor og brod, meaning butter and bread) is an icon of Danish food. These open-faced sandwiches, often made on a slice of rye bread, were initially created as a midday snack for blue-collar workers and farmers in the early days of industrialization. However, they have become a staple in the Danish diet over time. Children take these sandwiches to school, office goers take them for lunch, and even Michelin-starred restaurants serve their own high-end versions. They are made with a huge variety of toppings, so try some with your favorite ingredients.

Smorrebrod.

The Danish diet is high in fat and protein as the cold weather and demanding lifestyle calls for energy-rich and calorically dense food. However, the New Nordic Cuisine Movement has triggered a wave of modern-inspired recipes involving delicate and intricate cooking methods.

Copenhagen is a great place to enjoy other arts, including music. One of the most prominent festivals is the Copenhagen Jazz Festival, which highlights the city's jazz heritage and attracts a global audience. Numerous concert venues showcase a diverse range of genres and artists at the festival. Another well-known festival is the Copenhagen Fashion Week, which attracts designers, buyers, and fashion enthusiasts from every corner of the world.

Copenhagen is at the forefront of design, especially with architecture, furniture, and lifestyle products characterized by simplicity, functionality, and aesthetics. The Danes take pride in being expert craftsmen, working with some of the finest materials and crafting products using techniques that take decades to master.

SPORTS IN COPENHAGEN

Copenhagen features a wide variety of outdoor activities and sports, reflecting the city's focus on healthy living, sustainability, and enjoying the natural surroundings.

By far, the most popular activity is cycling. Copenhagen is known as one of the world's most bike-friendly cities. It features a massive network of bike lanes and has several programs supporting cycling, becoming intertwined with Danish culture. People cycle for work and leisure.

Even for visitors, cycling is the best way to explore the city in an eco-friendly manner. Cycling across the scenic Knippelsbro and Bryggebroen bridges is particularly enjoyable.

Copenhagen has easy access to clean water, and sailing and water activities are naturally very popular. In this re³gard, the Nyhavn waterfront and the Inner Harbor (Indre Havn) are popular spots for sailing, boating, kayaking, and other water-related activities.

'Harbor baths,' such as Brygge Harbor Bath and Amager Beachpark, are great for swimming, sunbathing, and enjoying the waterfront during the summer.

Copenhagen has parks and green spaces that are ideal for running, jogging, walking, and other outdoor fitness activities. For instance, the Soerne Lakes Loop, consisting of three lakes – Sankt Jorgens So, Peblinge So, and Sortedams So – Faelledparken, and Amager Faelled are popular for jogging and running. Also, you can find waterfront trails close to the Inner Harbor and Oresund Coast.

An annual marathon, the Copenhagen Marathon, attracts runners from all over the world. It's held in May and is a World Athletics Bronze Label race.

Other popular outdoor activity venues include Tivoli Gardens, Frederiksberg Have, and Orstedsparken, where you can enjoy picnics, yoga, and leisurely walks.

Winters in Copenhagen bring snow, and activities like ice skating, sledding, and cross-country skiing have become the norm. Also, you can enjoy wonderful winter events and cultural activities at the annual Frost Festival.

FAMOUS COPENHAGENERS

Here are a few famous individuals from Copenhagen.

Lars von Trier – Lars Von Trier is best known for his role as director of popular movies, including *Melancholia* and *Dancer in the Dark*. Hailing from Copenhagen, Trier is also a screenwriter and producer. His focus is usually on bringing to life complex themes through innovative storytelling techniques.

Lars Von Trier.[4]

Karen Blixen – Blixen is a writer commonly known by her pen name Isak Dinesen. Her most famous works include *Out of Africa* and *Seven Gothic Tales*. She was born in Rungstedlund, north of Copenhagen. Her writing was inspired by her experiences in Africa, Danish folklore, and other existential themes. One thing that sets her apart is her ability to explore human relationships in her writing and make them a central part of her creative endeavors. She is among the most highly regarded writers in Denmark.

Rene Redzepi – Redzepi is the mastermind behind the highly-rated restaurant Noma in Copenhagen. He has won multiple Michelin stars for the culinary masterpieces he creates at Noma. He focuses on bringing Nordic cuisine to life in the most authentic way possible using locally sourced and seasonal ingredients. His role at Noma and his overall contribution to the food industry have been significant in introducing Nordic cuisine to people visiting Copenhagen from all over the world.

Nikolaj Coster-Waldau – Born in Rudkobing, Nikolaj is a highly celebrated actor who recently achieved global recognition for his role as Jaime Lannister in the TV series 'Game of Thrones.' He has been an influential part of Danish cinema and appeared in many international films. Other titles he has acted in include *Oblivion* and *Shot Caller*.

Bjarke Ingels – Ingels is an architect and founder of the BIG (Bjarke Ingels Group) architecture firm. He led iconic development projects in Copenhagen, including the Copen-Hill Ski Slope and the 8-House Residential Complex. The BIG company played a leading role in the Amager Bakke Waste-to-Energy Plant.

Mads Dittmann Mikkelsen – Mads is a Danish actor, former gymnast, and dancer born in the Østerbro district of Copenhagen, best known for his role in the famous Netflix series Hannibal, an intense psychological drama. He also appeared in several notable movies: Fantastic Beasts: The Secrets of Dumbledore, Doctor Strange, and The Hunt.

Niels Bohr – Bohr is a Danish physicist, also known as "The Father of Modern Physics." Born in 1885 in Copenhagen, he made revolutionary contributions to the current understanding of atomic structure and quantum mechanics. He is best known for developing the Bohr model of the atom. In recognition of his innovative work, he was awarded the Nobel Prize in Physics in 1922.

Brigitte Nielsen – Famous as both a model and actress, Brigitte was born in Copenhagen in 1963. She began her career in modeling during her teenage years before switching to acting. She starred in Hollywood blockbuster movies like Rocky IV and Beverly Hills Cop II. In addition to her work in arts, she is also known for her involvement in sports. She was a member of the Danish National Women's Handball Team, which took home the 1996 European Championship.

TRANSPORT NETWORK

Copenhagen is extremely convenient to traverse – getting from one point to another is easy and efficient.

PUBLIC TRANSPORT

Copenhagen's public transport includes a metro, an S-train network, and local and harbor buses. The metro lines (M1, M2, M3, and M4) cover all the major areas, including the airport, city center, and suburbs.

The S-train network connects Copenhagen with surrounding regions and suburbs farther out. The best part of the S-train network is how it weaves into metro stations and bus stops so that travelers can quickly get onto another mode of transport to reach areas more centrally located in Copenhagen.

Movia operates an excellent local bus network. It covers all the main areas in Copenhagen and runs a night bus service. A branch of the bus network, the Harbor Bus system operates on a route covering the entire waterfront area, giving travelers a scenic view of the city and the shoreline.

CYCLING INFRASTRUCTURE

Cycling is the most common and most popular form of transport in Copenhagen. A big cycling-friendly infrastructure of bike lanes, cycling tracks, bike-friendly streets, and ride-sharing options facilitates cycling. Programs such as Donkey Republic make obtaining a bike easy. You can hire a bike where you need it and drop it off at a designated area.

WATER TRANSPORT

Copenhagen has water access at the harbor and several canals running through different parts of the city. You can use ferries and water buses to get to various places in these areas. The Copenhagen Harbor Bus (Havnebussen) service connects several harbor destinations.

RAIL LINKS

A robust train network centers around the Copenhagen Central Station. Trains connect to other cities, such as Aarhus and Aalborg, from here. You can catch trains that connect Copenhagen to international destinations, such as Malmo in Sweden, via the Oresund Bridge.

INTERNATIONAL CONNECTIONS

Copenhagen is home to Kastrup Airport, the largest airport in Scandinavia. This international gateway connects the city to the rest of the world and delivers an excellent domestic transportation system.

ESSENTIAL RESOURCES FOR COPENHAGEN

Here is a list of essential resources to make your travel to Copenhagen faster, easier, and more enjoyable.

TRANSPORT

+ *https://dinoffentligetransport.dk/en/plan-your-journey*
+ *https://intl.m.dk/travel-information/the-timetable/*
+ *https://international.kk.dk/live/transport-and-parking/public-transport/public-transport-in-copenhagen*
+ *https://moovitapp.com/index/en/public_transit-lines-Danmark-2965-1203484*
+ *https://www.visitcopenhagen.com/copenhagen/planning/public-transport*
+ *https://www.omio.com/train-stations/denmark/copenhagen/copenhagen-hemir*

HOTELS

+ *https://www.scandichotels.com/hotels/denmark/copenhagen?utm_source=google&utm_medium=cpc&utm_campaign=DK_Generic_EN&utm_id=19871642873&&cmpid=ppc_GH3nd&s_kwcid=AL!7589!3!66886069*

*6719!e!!g!!copenhagen%20hotels&gad_source=1&gcl
id=CjwKCAjw57exBhAsE
iwAaIxaZtfWuAYsD45hFtk5B1XZQzMbTcYIc
rILGmARmBm4ru0iZmTMKrz7rxoCAZUQAvD_BwE&gclsrc=aw.ds*

✦ *https://www.nh-hotels.com/en/hotel/nh-colle
ction-copenhagen?campid=8435708&gad_source=1&gclid
=CjwKCAjw57exBhAsEiwAaIxaZ
qay37Y7DvnlePFuK7IYcutDYkMy9eYoKCuhVWCL
J4SjgZlAlfO48RoCno8QAvD_BwE&gclsrc=aw.ds*

✦ *https://www.booking.com/city/dk/copenhagen.html*

✦ *https://www.tripadvisor.com/Hotels-g189541-Copenhagen_Zealand-
Hotels.html*

✦ *https://www.hotels.com/de408991/hotels-copen
hagen-denmark/?locale=en_IE&pos=HCOM_EMEA&siteid=300000025*

✦ *https://www.cntraveler.com/gallery/best-copenhagen-hotels*

LOCAL ATTRACTIONS

✦ *https://www.viator.com/Copenhagen/d463*

✦ *https://www.visitcopenhagen.com/copenhagen/a
ctivities/top-attractions-copenhagen*

✦ *https://www.tripadvisor.com/Attractions-g18954
1-Activities-Copenhagen_Zealand.html*

✦ *https://www.visitdenmark.com/denmark/things-d
o/attractions/copenhagen*

✦ *https://www.planetware.com/tourist-attractions-
/copenhagen-dk-z-cop.htm*

TO AND FROM THE KASTRUP AIRPORT

Welcome to Copenhagen Airport, known as Kastrup Airport, the largest international airport in the Nordic region and your gateway to Denmark. This airport has two main terminals, 2 and 3. Terminal 1 was closed in 2015. It services close to 27 million travelers yearly and is the main airport for Denmark and a regional gateway connecting the rest of the world to Scandinavian countries. Kastrup Airport is only 8 kilometers from Copenhagen city center, so it is a perfect starting point to explore the island of Zealand and the south of Denmark.

As you step into Copenhagen Airport, you'll be immersed in a world of seamless travel experiences. This modern and efficient airport features state-of-the-art facilities and convenient amenities. From the moment you arrive, the airport's clear signage, helpful staff, and streamlined processes ensure a smooth journey from check-in to boarding and beyond. This is particularly important because Kastrup Airport is a 'self-service' workflow. In most cases, you must perform several operations yourself at self-service e-gates. You will only see airport employees at the main points, such as immigration officers and security control personnel. This may seem cumbersome, but thanks to the airport's clean layout and workflow, it is easy to manage, even for first-time travelers.

Within the airport, you can explore a range of services tailored to enhance your travel experience. These services include spacious lounges offering shopping, dining, and relaxation opportunities. Whether embarking on a new adventure, returning home, or connecting to another destination, Copenhagen Airport provides everything for a comfortable and enjoyable journey. Moreover, the high organization level and easy access to services and amenities make navigating the airport simple and enjoyable.

Join the ranks of millions of travelers who have experienced the convenience and hospitality of Copenhagen Airport, where every detail will make your travel experience unforgettable.

TRANSPORT OPTIONS FROM THE AIRPORT

One of the main challenges travelers face at any airport is getting from the airport to the city center or the closest city or town. Kastrup Airport offers several quick, easy, and affordable options. Whether traveling solo, as a family with kids, or even as a large group, there will be an option that suits your needs. Here's a quick look at the main travel options to and from Kastrup Airport.

METRO

One of the easiest, fastest, and most economical is the metro train service, Metroselskabet. This train service runs 24 hours a day, 7 days a week, so no matter when you need to get to the airport, this is always an option. Moreover, the metro has a network of 39 stations that will take you to all the main locations in Copenhagen, including (on the M2 line) Frederiksberg, Norreport, and Nytorv. The same line will also take you to the city center of Copenhagen. It takes roughly 15-20 minutes to get to the city center from the airport.

REGIONAL TRAINS

Another railway option is the Danish State Railways (DSB), which connects the Copenhagen International Airport to various destinations within Denmark and Southern Sweden. You can find the DSB train station at Terminal 3 of the airport. If you plan to go to a different city from the airport, such as Malmo, Helsignor, or Roskilde, the DSB train is an excellent option.

BUS LINES

Several bus services operate in Denmark, connecting Copenhagen to the Kastrup Airport. The biggest operator is Movia, which connects Kastrup Airport to Copenhagen city and its surrounding areas.

You can find bus stops outside Terminals 2 and 3 at the airport, making access to a bus immediately after your flight convenient. It is a great option for people who want to go straight to a specific neighborhood or visit the city's main areas. Of course, these buses provide connections to other transportation hubs, so you can use them for the first leg of your journey if you are going to another city or one of the outside areas in Copenhagen.

TAXI SERVICES AND RIDE SHARING SERVICES

Copenhagen also has several taxi service operators, with Dantaxi and Taxa 4x35 being two of the most popular companies. At the airport, you will find designated taxi stands to easily book a taxi and be on your way directly to your destination.

Also, ride-sharing services, like Viggo, operate at the airport. It is a more affordable option than a private taxi and a great way to get to town if traveling with a group or if you don't mind sharing a taxi with a fellow traveler heading to the same destination.

If you want a direct and quick solution, a private taxi or a shared service is certainly a fantastic choice.

GENERAL TIPS

In addition to the transport options mentioned, here are additional tips for getting around more conveniently.

COPENHAGEN CARD FOR TRANSPORT

One of the most useful things you can invest in is the Copenhagen Card. It is like a bus card but packed with many other benefits. The card's main feature is transport. You get unlimited access to public transport, including buses, trains, and the metro. You can use this card within the city and to and from the airport. Moreover, this card gives you free access to the most popular attractions, and you can even get discounts at restaurants and certain shops. If you plan on using the public transport system extensively, this must-have will save you money in the long run.

TICKET COUNTERS

One of the best features of the Kastrup Airport is that all ticket counters for services like the Copenhagen Metro, regional trains, buses, and taxis are within the airport. Near Terminals 2 and 3, you'll find ticket counters to purchase tickets and information about routes and fares.

EXPECTED COSTS

Many variables determine how much it will cost to get from Kastrup Airport to Copenhagen, including time of day, mode of transport, amount of traffic, and how you pay. For instance, the Copenhagen Card may seem like a high price, but it is a payment for the card, not only for the trip from the airport to the city center.

Here is a general breakdown of how much you should expect to pay as of writing this book.

If you take the metro, you can expect to pay 30 Kr from the airport to the city center. Taking the bus will cost 30 Kr. A private taxi will cost roughly 250 Kr to 350 Kr.

HOURS OF SERVICE

Another significant benefit of the metro is the operating hours and frequency. The Copenhagen metro operates 24/7. During peak hours, such as in the afternoon, you can expect a train to arrive once every four minutes. In off-peak hours, for instance, from midnight to 5:45 am, you can expect a train at least 3 times an hour. These schedules ensure minimal wait times for passengers and manage congestion during peak hours.

On the other hand, regional trains and buses operate according to a fixed schedule, so the waiting times are a bit longer but are punctual and reliable. However, you have the flexibility of getting to more destinations, which is an excellent choice if you want to go to the city's suburbs and residential areas or the countryside. Visit the website or download the app to stay on top of your schedule so you can easily plan your trip. The app will give you real-time updates about service frequency changes or operational hours.

TIPS ON NAVIGATING THE AIRPORT

To make your experience as smooth and enjoyable as possible, here are a few key tips to help you navigate the airport.

First, you must familiarize yourself with the layout and key areas of the airport, including check-in counters, security checkpoints, departure lounges, and gates. Throughout the airport, you will find digital maps and screens showing you where you are and the rest of the airport's layout. Take a picture on your phone for additional convenience.

Signs and directions will guide you to amenities, transportation hubs, and service areas. No matter where you are, look around, and you will easily find directions and signs informing you about what is available around you.

Information desks and digital displays throughout the Kastrup Airport provide assistance and guidance. Flight information is on screens indicating gate changes and additional services when necessary.

3

INDRE BY: THE HEART OF THE CITY

BRIEF HISTORY OF INDRE BY

Indre By is the most central area of Copenhagen and is home to the Nyhavn Canal. It is the first settlement established in the 10th century when Vikings came to develop a small fishing village. During the latter part of the 12th century, the settlement grew significantly because of the fortress built on Slotsholmen by Bishop Absalon. In the 17th century, the city was further fortified with walls and gates to protect it from invasions and the core area of the Indre By settlement.

Indre By.[5]

Nearly three centuries after its inception, the town of Copenhagen, and specifically Indre By, had established itself as a major commercial trading hub, and areas such as Gammeltorv and Nytorv were well-known trading points.

Later, during the rule of King Christian IV, Indre By underwent extensive architectural growth and urban development. Key buildings such as Rosenborg Castle, the Round Tower, and the Borsen were constructed. Many of these historic buildings stand today and are operational. This development attracted people to Copenhagen and further established Indre By as one of the most prominent areas in the entire region, encapsulating Northern Europe and Scandinavia.

Rosenborg Castle.[6]

During the 17th century, developments such as the Rosenborg Castle Gardens and other amenities and services for residents made Copenhagen a popular city for people to immigrate to and visit as tourists.

Indre By has faced its fair share of problems, notably the Copenhagen Fire of 1728, which destroyed a large portion of the Indre By district. The area was rebuilt with wider streets and more fire-resistant buildings. During the early 19th century, the city faced plagues and was under siege by British forces. The city of Copenhagen has faced many wars, and Indre By has always been a prime target.

In the early 20th century, with the onset of industrialization, the city underwent a significant development increase. The city walls were removed to make room for further expansion with extensive urban renewal projects, and this relatively small town/settlement evolved into a modern city center and became the hub of the greater city of Copenhagen. Key infrastructural developments, such as the construction of the Central Station, also occurred.

Did You Know?

Copenhagen is home to two of the oldest amusement parks in the world, Tivoli and Bakken.

MAIN ATTRACTIONS

ROSENBORG CASTLE

Rosenborg Castle is one of the main attractions in Indre By, Copenhagen. The castle is open to the public, but the visiting hours vary according to the season, so check the operational hours on the official site before you visit. You can explore the castle and the surround-

ing gardens on your own or with a guided tour.

This castle is one of the finest examples of classic Danish architecture and is still in exceptional condition. Commissioned by King Christian IV and built between 1606 and 1634, it was King Christian IV's summer home and, for a time, also his permanent accommodation. The castle has been home to several monarchs and remained a residence for the royal family until the early 18th century.

Today, it houses a museum of artifacts depicting the fascinating history of the royal family, the nation's leaders, and some of the most prized possessions of the Danish empire, including royal artifacts, portraits, furniture, and personal belongings of distinguished individuals. There are also intricate historical tapestries depicting significant events in Danish history.

Rosenborg Castle was built in a distinctive Danish design characterized by symmetrical design, tall towers, and elaborate decorative elements. It is one of the finest examples of Renaissance architecture in Denmark.

As of the writing of this book, the Rosenborg Castle is open every day from 10 am to 5 pm. However, please make sure to double-check the opening hours should there be any changes to their schedule.

Address: Øster Voldgade 4A, 1350 København, Denmark.

THE ROUND TOWER (RUNDETAARN)

The Rundetaarn (Round Tower) is in the heart of Indre By and is an iconic landmark renowned for its historical significance, panoramic views, and architecture. This structure is another marvel constructed during the rule of King Christian IV, built between 1637 and 1642.

The Rundetaarn (Round Tower).[7]

King Christian IV was ambitious to make Copenhagen a center for astronomical study and scientific research. In this endeavor, he constructed the Rundetaarn as an astronomical observatory. This building was part of the Trinitatis Complex, which included a universal library and a church.

One of the most distinctive features is that this 36-meter-high tower has no stairs. Instead, it has a helical ramp that spirals 7.5 times around the hollow core to reach the observatory at the top, so horses and horse-drawn carriages can reach the top. The observatory at the top is the oldest functioning observatory in Europe and is still used today for research. It is open to the public, and you can enjoy panoramic views of the city of Copenhagen and, of course, the sky. On the second floor of the Trinitatis complex, a cultural center, a popular venue for exhibitions, events, and concerts.

As of the writing of this book, the opening hours are Thursday to Monday from 10 am to 6 pm and Tuesday and Wednesday from 10 am to 9 pm.

Address: Købmagergade 52A, 1150 København, Denmark

TRANSPORT

There are several ways to get around in the Indre By region. Here are some of the best options.

Metro – If you want to get from Indre By to other districts in the city or the Copenhagen Airport, then the Metro is a great choice. The Metro is efficient, running every few minutes during the day and every 10-20 minutes at night.

Buses – Since Indre By is a central part of the city, plenty of bus routes are available to get around the area and to see the local attractions, such as Tivoli Gardens, Christiansborg Palace, and Nyhavn. Buses are quick, efficient, and a great way to get around Indre By or reach other parts of Copenhagen.

S-Tog – Norreport station is a major hub for S-Tog lines. These trains are a great way to get to the suburbs of Copenhagen or other areas outside of the main city.

S-Tog lines.[8]

Harbor Buses – There is no option more scenic than the harbor buses. These water buses operate along the Copenhagen Harbor and are a great way to get from one part of Indre By to another.

Bicycles – Cycling is Copenhagen's most popular form of transport, and Indre By is no exception. There are plenty of bike lanes and places to rent a bike or get a bike-sharing option.

E-Bikes – For something slightly less physically taxing, get a public electric bike. There are multiple docking stations in the city. You can rent a bike through the app or directly from a docking station.

Walking – To truly enjoy the area's hidden gems and narrow streets, then get around on foot. Many of the main squares and streets, like Stroget, are pedestrian-only zones. Indre By is not very big, so you can easily cover the area on foot.

Taxis – Taxis are plentiful in the area. You can hail a taxi on the street, a taxi rank, or book through an app. If you have kids or luggage and need transport to your destination, this is a great option.

EXPERIENCES

Tivoli Gardens – Tivoli Gardens was opened in 1843, making it one of the oldest amusement parks in the world. This iconic setup is home to thrilling rides, beautiful gardens, live entertainment, and delicious food. It's a one-stop solution for anyone looking for a good time. Depending on when you go, you can experience seasonal decorations. It is famous for its Halloween decorations. The beautiful gardens, rides, shows, live performances, and wide range of Danish and international food stalls and restaurants make it a must-visit spot for any traveler.

Tivoli Gardens entrance.[9]

Address: Vesterbrogade 3, 1630 København V, Denmark

FREDERIKS KIRKE (CHURCH)

Frederik's Church is located at the center of Old Town Copenhagen near Amalienborg Palace. It is a combination of historic and modern art architecture. This grand marble Baroque church remained incomplete from 1770 until 1874 and was finally completed in 1894. The entry is free of charge, and the interior is breathtaking. It is a lovely place to go when you want a break from the city, a place where you can relax, meditate, or pray. There is a rooftop dome tour every day at 1 PM but it only allows fifteen people.

Frederik's Church.[10]

Address: Frederiksgade 4, Copenhagen 1265 Denmark

Climbing Rundetaarn – The Round Tower is an outstanding experience. The spiral ramp leading to the top of the building (the observatory) is worth exploring. On your way to the top, you can stop at the cultural center to enjoy different events, concerts, and exhibitions.

Streets – Copenhagen is proactive regarding eco-friendliness and reducing carbon emissions. Many streets are dedicated pedestrian-only zones. For instance, Stroget is one of Europe's longest pedestrian shopping streets. Besides, exploring these scenic and historic locations on foot is the best way to soak in the atmosphere and enjoy the scenes more comfortably.

FAMILY FUN

National Museum of Denmark – The National Museum of Denmark houses an extensive collection of Danish history from the Stone Age to the present day. More importantly, it features interesting artifacts from other cultures around the world. It has interactive exhibits igniting the imagination of adults and children, making it an educational and enjoyable experience. Some of the main things to see at the museum include Viking exhibits, Danish Prehistory, and cultural artifacts. Other interesting things are weapons, tools, and even ships from days past. The museum features special exhibits, so check the museum's site before you visit.

National Museum of Denmark.[11]

Address: Ny Vestergade 10, 1471 København K, Denmark

THE HIRSCHSPRUNG COLLECTION

The Hirschsprung Collection is a very valuable collection any art lover would be delighted to visit. The collection is the personal art collection of Heinrich Hirschsprung, who was a tobacco manufacturer. He donated his collection to the Danish state in 1902, and since then, this personal collection of some of the best Danish art pieces has been made available to the public. Specifically, the collection focuses on 19th-century and early 20th-century art pieces and are some of the best examples of the Danish Golden Age. Here, you will find works from some of the greatest names in Danish art including Eckersberg, Kroyer, Kobke, and Hammershoi, to name a few. It is located in a beautiful building in the Ostre Anlaeg park.

The Hirschsprung Collection building.[12]

Address: Stockholmsgade 20, 2100 København, Denmark

Amalienborg Museum

The Amalienborg Museum is a unique opportunity to explore Denmark's rich royal history over the past two and a half centuries. At Christian VIII's Palace, you can get a glimpse of what royal life looked like today and in the past. You can also access the royal reception rooms of past monarchs. If you love architecture and history, Amalienborg Museum is worth a visit. It is also close to New Haven and New Harbor, which you can visit as your next destination after enjoying Amalienborg.

Amalienborg Museum.[13]

Address: Christian VIII's Palæ, Amalienborg Slotsplads 5, 1257 København, Denmark

WHERE TO EAT

Noma - Located at Refshalevej 96, Noma is the brainchild of world-renowned chef Rene Redzepi. This establishment focuses on Nordic cuisine, and its unique feature is its innovative reinventing Nordic classics. This world-class restaurant has been named the best restaurant in the world multiple times. Their best menu items include sea urchin and walnut and beef tartare with ants – although they do change with the season.

Address: Refshalevej 96, 1432 Indre By, Denmark.

Aamanns 1921 – Located at Niels Hemmingsens Gade 19-21, Aamanns head chef, Adam Aamann, focuses on the classic Nordic dish, *smorrebrod* (open-faced sandwiches). While otherwise considered the average man's meal, at Aamanns this dish has elevated to gourmet levels. Some of the best menu options include herring smorrebrod, beetroot tartare, and chicken salad smorrebrod.

Address: Niels Hemmingsens Gade 19-21, 1153 København K, Denmark

Restaurant Karla – Located at the corner of Dantes Plades and Vester Volgade this is a popular local establishment selling Danish classics. Some of the best things to try here include the shrimp cocktail, roast pork, and open-face sandwiches. Here, you will also find a full bar, so be sure to try some of the local beers with your food. In summer, the restaurant also has outdoor seating, which offers a fantastic street view of the surrounding area.

Address: Dantes Plads 1, 1556 København V, Denmark

SANKT PEDERS BAGERI

Sankt Peders Bageri is a must-visit bakery in Copenhagen that serves delicious Danish pastries, including light sugar-dusted muffins filled with rich chocolate cream, buttery croissants with ramekins and vanilla mascarpone cream topped with fresh berries, and delicious cinnamon buns. The staff is friendly and always happy to help. The place has cozy vibes, and the fresh smell of pastries makes customers come back every time.

Address: Sankt Peders Stræde 29, Copenhagen 1453 Denmark

MAPLE CASUAL DINING

Maple Casual Dining is a cozy, family-friendly restaurant that serves homemade, international, and European cuisine. People love their tasty food, friendly service, and relaxed vibes. The menu includes delicious dishes such as duck confit, perfectly cooked sea bass, juicy steak, and flavorful ribs served with a rich sauce. It also has vegetarian, vegan, and gluten-free options to support everyone's preferences. If you are looking for the perfect after-work drink, order the standout spicy margaritas. Whether you want to enjoy a casual dinner or celebrate a special occasion, Maple Casual Dining is an excellent choice.

Address: Vesterbrogade 24, 1620 København, Denmark

TANGO Y VINOS

Tango y Vinos is a steakhouse, grill, and wine bar that operates by the concept of food, wine, and music. You have the option to choose between indoor or outdoor seating to enjoy their live music performance. It is a lovely place for couples to enjoy a romantic date night. They have a good wine list that you can enjoy with their perfectly cooked steak! There is free Wi-Fi, credit cards, and gift cards available.

Address: Herluf Trolles Gade 9, Copenhagen 1052 Denmark

SHOPPING GUIDE

Stroget – Stroget is a pedestrian-only shopping street and one of the longest in Europe, extending to over 1 km. It starts at the City Hall Square (Rådhus-pladsen) and ends at Kongens Nytorv. Here, you will find a wide variety of stores with super high-end options, such as Gucci, Prada, and Louis Vuitton, and other more familiar brands, such as H&M and Zara.

Stroget is a pedestrian-only shopping street.[14]

Address: Strøget 29, 23, 1164 København, Denmark

Illum - Illum is a premium department store great for everyday needs and high-end versions of daily-use items. The store in Indre By is at Ostergade 52 near Stroget. Here, you will find a range of high-end fashion products, beauty products, accessories, and other goods. The building's top floor houses a selection of gourmet restaurants and cafes with stunning views of the city of Copenhagen.

Address: Østergade 52, 1100 København, Denmark

Magasin du Nord - This store in Indre By is at Kongens Nytorv 13, an iconic department store since 1868. It offers a wide range of goods, including beauty products, home decor items, gourmet food, and international and local Danish brands. The basement hosts a gourmet food hall where you can pick up many local and international delicacies. Best of all, it offers tax-free shopping for tourists.

Address: Kongens Nytorv 13, 1095 København K, Denmark

ENTERTAINMENT

Nyhavn – Nyhavn is one of Copenhagen's oldest and finest entertainment areas in Copenhagen. A historic waterfront initially developed in the 17th century, the area features a canal and an extensive entertainment district lined with colorful townhouses, various bars, cafes, restaurants, and entertainment outlets. The picturesque setting and the lively and vibrant atmosphere make this a charming place to enjoy live music and excellent local cuisine and experience the culture like a native.

Nyhavn.[15]

For an exciting experience, take a boat tour down the canal with countless places to take captivating photographs of colorful buildings, old ships, and people having an amazing time.

Address: Indre By, Denmark

The Royal Danish Theatre – The Royal Danish Theatre in Kongens Nytorv is a premium venue for performing arts in Copenhagen. The three main stages/venues are the Old Stage (Gamle Scene), the Opera House, and the Royal Danish Playhouse. The theater hosts a range of performances, including opera, ballet, classical concerts, contemporary plays, and much more. It is home to the Royal Danish Ballet, one of the world's oldest ballet companies. Apart from performances, the different stages are sights worth seeing as they are architectural masterpieces.

The Royal Danish Theatre in Kongens Nytorv.[16]

Address: August Bournonvilles Passage 8, 1055 København K, Denmark

SPORTS AND LEISURE

Cycling – Copenhageners love cycling. They use it for work and play. In Copenhagen, you have multiple cycling options. It is one of the most bike-friendly cities in the world. There are plenty of routes, and renting a bike through private or city-provided services is easy.

Running – Denmark has been at the forefront of eco-friendly movements and supporters of using alternative transport solutions to minimize carbon emissions. Running and walking are encouraged, and like their strong cycling infrastructure, there are many walkways and running tracks. These tracks are near scenic routes for a great view of the city and waterfronts. Tracks that run through The King's Garden and those near the Copenhagen Lakes (Soerne) are especially beautiful. The city is home to multiple running events and races throughout the year, so there are plenty of training tracks if you run competitively.

Kayaking and Paddleboarding – being so close to pristine water bodies, it's no surprise that boating, kayaking, and paddleboarding are extremely popular. However, these activities are best in the warmer months, as winter temperatures fall below freezing. The canals and waterfront area are great for water activities. Here, you can enjoy water tours through the harbor areas and canals. Multiple companies offer boats of all sizes, paddleboards, or kayaks to rent.

ACCOMMODATION

Hotels – In the Indre By area, multiple hotel options range from high-end 5-star hotels to more modestly priced 4- and 3-star options. Most hotels are centrally located, with excellent access to major attractions and transport options. Enjoy excellent service quality with top-of-the-line amenities.

Wakeup Copenhagen, Bernstrorffsgade Address: Bernstorffsgade 35, 1577 København, Denmark

Scandic Norreport Address: Frederiksborggade 18, 1360 København, Denmark

Manon Les Suites Address: Gyldenløvesgade 19, 1600 København V, Denmark

Apartments – If you are staying longer or need to house a larger group, renting an apartment could be a great option. Many options are available depending on the location and the size of the apartment. This way, you get privacy and a reasonable price, but you must manage your amenities, such as cooking, washing, and other services.

By the Lakes Apartments Address: Dahlerupsgade 3, 1603 København, Denmark

Ascot Apartments Address: Studiestræde 69, 1609 København, Denmark

Hostels – Hostels are an excellent option for people on a budget. You get a comfortable space to stay, but you must forgo things like breakfast and other in-house conveniences due to the lower price. In some hostels, you may get communal spaces for accommodation and social activities. These community-based hostels are the most cost-effective.

Steel House Copenhagen Address: Herholdtsgade 6, 1605 København V, Denmark

Danhostel Copenhagen City Address: H. C. Andersens Blvd. 50, 1553 København, Denmark

Copenhagen Downtown Hostel Address: Vandkunsten 5, 1467 København, Denmark

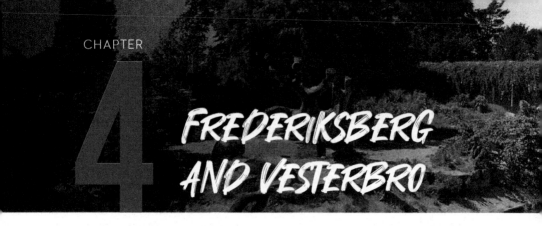

4 FREDERIKSBERG AND VESTERBRO

A BIT ABOUT FREDERIKSBERG AND VESTERBRO

Frederiksberg traces its origins to the 17th century when Dutch farmers occupied the area. In 1651, the area accommodated Dutch peasants housed at the nearby Amager Island. During this era, King Frederik III granted these farmers land (now Frederiksberg) to farm, and their produce was primarily used in the royal household. During this time, Frederiksberg was called Ny Hollaenderby (New Dutchman-Town).

Later in the 18th century, King Frederick IV built the Frederiksberg Palace as a summer residence. This structure and the surrounding gardens became a focal point and attracted additional regional development.

Frederiksberg Palace.[17]

Since its inception, Frederiksberg has maintained its position as an independent municipality. Today, Copenhagen surrounds the area, yet its unique status has allowed it to develop independently and establish itself as a prime residential area. The area's design, layout, and development have made it a sought-after residential location for the most affluent citizens. Even today, the wide streets, extensive green areas, and individualistic buildings set it apart from other areas in Copenhagen. Frederiksberg is home to several top-tier educational institutions, such as the Copenhagen Business School, cultural attractions, museums, and theaters.

Vesterbro shares a border with Frederiksberg, yet it is quite different from Frederiksberg. Vesterbro's growth and history is closely tied with Copenhagen's expansion, particularly the city's industrial development. Initially, it was a residential area outside the city's Western Gate. During the industrial boom in the 19th century, the gates were removed to gain more space for growth. Vesterbro took root when industrial buildings, factories, and other large-scale commercial endeavors started. Due to this development, the surroundings became a prime residential area for working-class workers employed in these industries.

Did You Know?

The Frederiksborg Castle, in Hillerød, was rebuilt in 1859 after a devastating fire.

By the mid-20th century, Vesterbro faced many typical issues in industrial urban areas, such as social problems and overcrowding. In the 1990s, the area underwent a radical transformation aimed at improving living conditions and infrastructure.

In the 21st century, this wave of change continued when many old industrial buildings were repurposed into modern apartments, cultural venues, art galleries, and more. The area saw an influx of young professionals, including artists and entrepreneurs.

Today, Vesterbro is considered one of Copenhagen's most diverse districts, and it is known for its cultural attractions, lively nightlife, and unique mix of old and new. Kodbyen (Meatpacking District) is an example of how a previously rough area transformed into a hub for creative industries, nightlife, and fine dining.

FREDERIKSBERG PALACE

The Frederiksberg Palace, commissioned by King Frederick IV in the 18th century, is an outstanding baroque palace that was the royal residence. Over time, the palace was home to different monarchs and the nation's leaders.

Today, the palace houses the Royal Danish Military Academy. However, many parts of it are open to the public, where you can avail guided tours and learn about the structure's royal history, design, and architecture. The palace features baroque architecture, grand halls, and opulent interiors with expansive views of the surrounding gardens.

As of the writing of this book, the Frederiksberg Palace is open every day from 10 am to 5 pm. However, please double-check the opening hours should there be any changes to their schedule.

Address: Roskildevej 28 A, 2000 Frederiksberg C, Denmark

FREDERIKSBERG HAVE (FREDERIKSBERG GARDENS)

The Frederiksberg Gardens is one of Copenhagen's largest and most beautiful parks, surrounding the Frederiksberg Palace. This large green area seems like a bubble of nature in the middle of a very happening urban city.

The Frederiksberg Gardens.[18]

You'll find landscaped lawns, lakes, canals, and tree-lined paths. Some key features of this garden include the Chinese Pavilion, the grotto, and the Apis Temple.

As of the writing of this book, the opening hours are every day from 6 am to 9 pm. However, please double-check the opening hours should there be any changes to their schedule.

Address: 2000 Frederiksberg, Denmark

COPENHAGEN ZOO

Copenhagen Zoo is one of the oldest zoos in the world. It was founded in 1859 and is across from Frederiksberg. It is home to over 3000 animals from all over the world, including penguins, bears, lions, elephants, and polar bears.

Copenhagen Zoo.[19]

The zoo is well-known for its leading role in animal conservation and education. The zoo has dedicated children's play areas and many interactive exhibits that help educate visitors about animals and wildlife.

As of the writing of this book, the opening hours are every day from 9 am to 5 pm. However, please make sure to double-check the opening hours online should there be any slight changes to their schedule.

Address: Roskildevej 32, 2000 Frederiksberg, Denmark

KODBYEN (MEATPACKING DISTRICT)

As the name implies, Kodbyen was once home to slaughterhouses, packing plants, meat processing factories, and lamp oil production plants (which required animal byproducts as raw material). Since then, the neighborhood transformed, and since 2000, the area has been the focus of drastic urbanization efforts. Previously, this area faced many social and health-related problems due to the poor design and congested layout.

Today, it has evolved from a rough industrial area to one of the city's most modern and trendy neighborhoods. Here, you will find bars, art galleries, restaurants, and several nightlife venues. Whether you are looking for a delicious street-side snack or a gourmet dining experience, it's all available in Kodbyen. The development of art galleries and cultural centers has made it a hub for creativity and contemporary culture.

Kodbyen.[20]

As of the writing of this book, you can visit Kodbyen at any time during your trip. However, please make sure to double-check the opening hours online should there be any slight changes to their schedule.

CARLSBERG BREWERY

Carlsberg is one of the biggest global brands of mass-produced alcoholic beer. The original factory was founded in Vesterbro in 1847 and is a major landmark today. It has been significant in the area's development and Copenhagen's industrial history as one of the largest beer producers in the world.

You can visit the Carlsberg Visitor Center and tour the brewery to learn about the plant's history and the Carlsberg brand's heritage. Moreover, you can get an insider's peek into the brewing process, see historic brewing facilities, and enjoy beer tastings.

The surrounding area, the Carlsberg City District, is undergoing redevelopment, turning it into a modern urban area that will house residential buildings, offices, shops, and cultural venues.

As of the writing of this book, the opening hours are every day from 10 am to 8 pm. However, please make sure to double-check the opening hours online should there be any slight changes to their schedule.

Address: Gamle Carlsberg Vej 11, 1799 København, Denmark

ISTEDGADE

Istedgade is the main street in Vesterbro, offering the best of Vesterbro in every sense. Here, you will find some of the finest restaurants, cafes, bars, and multiple shopping options, from boutique stores to vintage shops. It is often the venue for cultural events and other activities in the neighborhood. Istedgade has a dynamic personality reflecting the neighborhood's diverse character.

Istedgade.[21]

TRANSPORT

CYCLING

Like other areas of Copenhagen, Vesterbro and Frederiksberg have an excellent cycling infrastructure with dedicated bike lanes and parking areas. Cycling is a great way to get around these neighborhoods. You can find bike rental shops throughout the city and multiple bike-sharing programs, like Donkey Republic, to get flexible and affordable bike rentals.

Consider a guided bike tour that will take you through the main highlights of the Vesterbro and Frederiksberg areas. These tours are a great way to learn about the historical and cultural significance of the various sites.

ELECTRIC SCOOTERS

Electric scooters are quickly becoming a popular mode of transport in the city and are especially useful for areas like Vesterbro, where traffic can be problematic. Multiple companies offer electric scooters for rent.

Primary electric scooter providers include Lime and Voi. You can find and unlock scooters through the app and start your journey. These are cost-effective, quick, and convenient, reducing carbon emissions.

PUBLIC TRANSPORT (BUS AND METRO)

Frederiksberg and Vesterbro are well served by the public transport systems. In these neighborhoods, plenty of bus and metro stations will quickly take you to many parts of these neighborhoods or other parts of the city.

The metro is particularly useful for getting to a distant location in the city or going to a different part of the country. Moreover, these transport options give you easy access to some of the main attractions in the Frederiksberg and Vesterbro areas.

EXPERIENCES

CISTERNERNE

Cisternerne is a fascinating art exhibition space. It was previously an underground water storage facility, so it has fascinating architecture, cool, dark, and quiet, and offers unusual acoustics. Today, this is a sought-after art gallery in the art world. It allows viewers to immerse themselves in art while enjoying the gallery's ambiance.

Given the gallery's history and the location, it is ideal for art pieces relating to water, environment, and history. Cisternerne is an excellent destination for art lovers interested in the intersection of art and natural elements.

Cisternerne.[22]

Address: Roskildevej 25A, 2000 Frederiksberg, Denmark

MIKKELLER BAR

Mikkeller bar, located in Vesterbro, is the original Mikkeller Bar co-founded and operated by Mikkel Borg Bjergso. In a past life, Mikkell was a school teacher and a homebrewer. In a short span of time, his brews became very popular and led him to establish Mikkeller bar where he serves primarily his own brews along with some brews from the top breweries in the world. Here, you will also find a good selection of bottles along with plenty to snack on including cheese, bread, meat, and other options as well. Mikkeller has earned himself an excellent reputation as a gypsy brewer as he travels to breweries across Denmark, Europe, and the United States to play a role in their brewing process. Mikkeller also owns several other beer bars and restaurants in Copenhagen and other cities around the world with different names. The original, however, is the Mikkeller Bar in Vesterbro.

Address: Viktoriagade 8, B-C, 1655 København, Denmark

DET NY TEATER

The Det Ny Teater is one of the largest in Denmark. It was opened in 1908 and has been operational since then. In the mid 1980's it was closed for renovation and was back to serving clients in 1994. The theater is located in a historic building which covers 12,000 square meters making it one of the largest theaters in Europe as well. The theater is best known for playing musicals and theater performances, including titles such as *Les Miserables*, *Evita*, and *Billy Elliot: The Musical*.

The Det Ny Teater.[23]

Address: Gl. Kongevej 29, 1610 København, Denmark

Copenhagen Skatepark – One of North Europe's largest indoor skateparks, it caters to BMX riders, rollerbladers, and skateboarders. You can enjoy watching local talent perform impressive tricks and stunts, or you can rent equipment and have a go yourself. The skatepark has a shop selling skate gear and equipment and a cafe for refreshments. It is a fantastic place for children and adults with different tracks catering to all skill levels.

Address: Enghavevej 80, 2450 København, Denmark

FAMILY FUN

CARLSBERG CITY DISTRICT

The Carlsberg City District is an interesting blend of historical brewery buildings and modern urban development. It is a great place to explore as a family, with much to see and learn. When visiting the factory, don't miss the iconic Elephant Gate and participate in the interactive exhibits. This area has family-friendly events and many open spaces for children to play. The unique combination of cultural heritage and modern amenities make it a fantastic location for all ages.

Elephant Gate.[24]

SONDER BOULEVARD

Sonder Boulevard is a vibrant and family-friendly boulevard in Vesterbro, ideal for outdoor activities and quality time with the people you love most. Here, you will find large, open green spaces, recreational areas, and playgrounds.

Various playgrounds facilitate different age groups with other facilities, such as basketball courts, table tennis tables, and solutions for other games and activities. Several cafes nestle along the boulevard, where you can get a bite to eat and enjoy a picnic in the green areas.

Sonder Boulevard.[25]

COPENHAGEN ZOO

The Copenhagen Zoo is one of Europe's oldest and finest zoos. Some key attractions include the Elephant House, Arctic Ring, Tropical Zoo, Children's Zoo, Savannah Exhibit, and a section for Nordic Animals. The zoo is extensively involved in multiple conservation efforts locally and internationally. Copenhagen Zoo is involved in several breeding programs for endangered animals and collaborates with other institutions on wildlife preservation efforts.

Other than seeing animals, the zoo provides a complete day-out experience with restaurants, picnic areas, and gift shops. If traveling with kids or seniors, Stroller rentals and accessible pathways accommodate visitors with mobility challenges or if traveling with kids.

Oksnehallen

Oksnehallen is a historic building in the Vesterbro area, which in the past used to be an indoor cattle market but today has been repurposed to be an exhibition center and conference venue. The structure was built in 1899 and since then has gone through several phases of reconstruction and development while keeping the essence of the structure the same. Apart from the art that is on exhibition there, the location and the historic building itself are worth a visit. Currently, it is the largest venue of its kind in Copenhagen.

Oksnehallen.[26]

Address: Halmtorvet 11, 1700 København, Denmark

WHERE TO EAT

Mielcke and Hurtigkarl – This top-tier restaurant in the picturesque Frederiksberg Gardens is well-known for its artistic and innovative approach to Danish cuisine. The restaurant has an ever-changing menu showcasing seasonal ingredients and the chef's culinary expertise.

Address: Frederiksberg Runddel 1, 2000 Frederiksberg, Denmark

Granola – This nostalgic cafe on Vaernedamsvej Street has a classic 1930s vibe. It has a cozy interior with vintage furniture and styling. Their best dish is the Brunch Plate, a delicious assortment of eggs, cheese, ham, fresh fruit, and yogurt. It is an excellent meal for a relaxed morning, matching the cafe's relaxed and laid-back atmosphere.

Address: Værnedamsvej 5, 1819 København, Denmark

Cafe Dyrehaven – This establishment on Sonder Boulevard is popular with locals. Initially, it was a traditional Danish pub. Today, it has been refurbished into a modern cafe but retains its historic charm. Their best dish is the Smorrebrod (open-faced sandwiches), available with a range of toppings, such as roast beef, shrimp, herring, cheese, ham, and much more. For a classic Danish Smorrebrod sandwich, this is the place to go.

Address: Sønder Blvd. 72, 1720 Vesterbro, Denmark

ALLEGADE 10

Located near Copenhagen Zoo and Frederiksberg Gardens, this one-of-a-kind European Scandinavian restaurant has a cozy, pet-friendly atmosphere with indoor and outdoor seating options. You can enjoy a casual breakfast, lunch, or a late-night meal with your friends. Guests like to unwind on warm summer evenings with drinks in the courtyard or garden. The interior is decorated with royal photos and paintings that make you feel like you are part of history.

Address: Allegade 10, 2000 Frederiksberg, Denmark

SATANG THAI BISTRO

Satang Thai Bistro is a small, intimate restaurant with cozy, inviting vibes that offers authentic Asian and Thai dishes with vegetarian-friendly options like papaya salad. The service is over the top, and the owners are super friendly. It is known for its fresh, flavorful dishes like the Massaman curry, chicken with green curry, steak and vegetables, and duck larb, with their best dish: the pad Thai. The restaurant is always busy, so make sure to make a reservation before you go to ensure availability.

Address: Aaboulevard 51, Frederiksberg, Copenhagen 1960 Denmark

DELIGRECO

Deligreco is a Greek restaurant near Frederiksberg City Hall. It serves amazing food with many plates to choose from at affordable prices. The staff is professional, friendly, and not in a rush. If you want to enjoy a drink, order the red wine because it is high-quality and tasty, you can't miss it. If you have food allergies and want to go somewhere safe, Deligreco is your go-to restaurant. They accommodate their dishes based on your preferences; just inform the waiter, and you're good to go.

Address: Gammel Kongevej 170, Frederiksberg, Copenhagen 1850 Denmark

SHOPPING GUIDE

Istedgade – Istedgade is one of the most well-known streets in Vesterbro and is regarded as one of the best shopping areas in the district. This street starts from the central train station and runs through the heart of Vesterbro. You will find a mix of vintage stores, boutique shops, and trendy clothing boutiques. Whether you are looking for high fashion, accessories, or home decor, you can find it here.

You also have access to some of the best cafes and bars in the district. There are several great food options to explore that will keep you fuelled during your shopping adventures.

Dora – Dora is one of the finest stores to visit if you are looking for home accessories. Here, you will find things for the bedroom, home office, kitchen, and bathroom. Their inventory is ever-evolving, and sometimes you can find lighting, rugs, and small decorations for the home. You never know what you will find at Dora, but you always know it will be well worth a visit. This is a reassuring trove and will certainly interest people looking for decoration, soft furnishings, and antique pieces.

Address: Værnedamsvej 6, 1619 København, Denmark

Frederiksberg Shopping Center – In the heart of Frederiksberg, this modern shopping mall offers a wide range of shops and services. It is a one-stop window for all your shopping needs. The mall houses over 90 stores, including multiple international brands, electronics, beauty stores, and Danish fashion retailers. Here, you can find everything from clothing and accessories to home goods and groceries.

Address: Falkoner Alle 21, 2000 Frederiksberg, Denmark

The best souvenirs can often be found at the local markets in this square. The choice of handmade goods, fresh local produce, and interesting handcrafts are unrivaled. For entertainment, you will find local performers you can watch from the comfort of outdoor seating areas. It's a fantastic place to get a taste of what local life is like for residents.

ENTERTAINMENT

Aveny T – Aveny T in Frederiksberg is a popular performing arts theater offering a wide variety of performances, including musicals, dance shows, stand-up comedy, and contemporary plays. It is one of the few venues accommodating local and international productions, catering to all age groups. It is a great place for tourists to experience Danish culture through the performing arts.

Address: Frederiksberg Allé 102, 1820 Frederiksberg, Denmark

Vega – In the heart of Vesterbro, Vega is Copenhagen's premier venue for live music performances. It has hosted local and international artists across various genres. The building is a historic gem, adding to the charm and ambiance of concerts. It has two main halls – Lille Vega and Store Vega. Each has a different atmosphere, depending on the size of the performance and audience. On regular days, Vega doubles as a nightclub venue and hosts DJs, making it a central location for nightlife and entertainment in Vesterbro.

Address: Enghavevej 40, 1674 København, Denmark

SPORTS AND LEISURE

Frederiksberg Swimming Baths – This is a historic and beautiful swimming complex. Opened in 1934, it features stunning architecture and a range of facilities. Here, you will find a full-sized pool with diving boards, great for casual swimming and doing laps, and a smaller pool for children. There is a sauna onsite, multiple fitness classes you can join, and an aerobics section, wellness treatments, and massages. It's a great place for exercise and relaxation.

Address: Helgesvej 29, 2000 Frederiksberg, Denmark

Vesterbro Running Club – This is a friendly and inclusive running group developed by Vesterbro's local community that organizes regular runs throughout the Vesterbro area. It is an excellent option for exploring the district on foot. The club's routes cover nearly all the scenic roads in the district. Moreover, it's a great way to meet and interact with the local community.

ACCOMMODATION

Serviced Apartments - A serviced apartment will be a great choice if you need space for a family or a group. Their rates vary depending on location. You get privacy and can use the accommodation as you would your home. Ideally, you want a place that is close to transport.

Cabinn Address: Arne Jacobsens Allé 4, 2300 København, Denmark

NABO Hotel Apartments Address: Korsgade 60, 2200 København, Denmark

Hotels - The area has many excellent hotels ranging from 5-star to more modestly priced ones. Hotels are a great option if you stay in a central area. Some hotels may be pricey, but you get outstanding service and an excellent place to unwind and relax.

Scandic Falkoner Address: Falkoner Alle 9, 2000 Frederiksberg, Denmark

Comfort Hotel Vesterbro Address: Vesterbrogade 23/29, 1620 København, Denmark

Communal Hostels - A communal hostel is the best choice for backpackers and solo travelers. Found throughout the Frederiksberg and Vesterbro area, they are the most cost-effective accommodation. You can get private rooms in some hostels but the most economical option will be a shared option.

CityHub Address: Vesterbrogade 97B, 1620 København, Denmark

Sleep in Heaven Address: Struenseegade 7, 2200 København, Denmark

Globalhagen Hostel Address: Ravnsborggade 11, 2200 København, Denmark

CHAPTER

5

OSTERBRO AND NORDRE FRIHAVN

A BIT ABOUT OSTERBRO AND NORDRE FRIHAVN

Osterbro, which translates to "Eastern Bridge," is one of the most affluent neighborhoods in the city. It sits on the eastern facet of Copenhagen and is home to some of the priciest real estate in the city. Originally, this was a rural part of Copenhagen used for agriculture, small cottage industries, and low-income housing. It was outside the city gates but expanded beyond its gated boundary as the city grew and became an integral part of the city.

In the late 19th century, Osterbro boomed. Wealthy residents from Copenhagen and other parts of the country moved to this part of the city during this time. The area offered space, wide boulevards, and proximity to green spaces and lakes, making it an ideal location.

Today, the area has kept many key traits that initially made it an attractive location. Considered one of the city's best residential areas, it offers residents an excellent quality of life.

Nordre Frihavn translates to "Northern Freeport." This city has a proud maritime history, and life here closely connects seafaring activities. This area was crucial in the 19th century when it was developed to extend Copenhagen's existing facilities to provide additional space for shipping and industrial activities.

Over time, shipping technologies evolved, and the Danish economy moved from industrialization to the services sector. The need for industrial developments in the area died down and was replaced by urban residential developments. Existing industrial structures were repurposed into residential and commercial structures. Today, many old buildings have been refurbished into trendy apartments, offices, and cultural venues.

Both areas have evolved from being used for military and industrial to residential, commercial, and cultural purposes. You will find excellent historical sites, fascinating natural views, and a hip and happening modern lifestyle here.

Did You Know?

Osterbro is home to one of the best-preserved military bases in Northern Europe, The Citadel (Kastellet).

MAIN ATTRACTIONS

The Lakes (Soerne) – The Lakes, locally known as Soerne, consist of three lakes stretching through several city districts, including Osterbro. The lakes are, Sortedams So, Peblinge So, and Sankt Jorgens So. They are surrounded by pedestrian and cycling tracks, making them ideal for jogging, walking, and cycling. They are the perfect getaway from the hustle and bustle of city life because of their proximity. The scenic views are stunningly beautiful during spring and summer when the grass is green and the flora is in full bloom.

Soerne.[27]

As of the writing of this book, you can visit the Lakes at any time during your visit.

The Little Mermaid Statue – The Little Mermaid Statue is one of Copenhagen's best-known iconic landmarks in the Langelinie promenade, Osterbro. The statue was commissioned by Carl Jacobsen, the son of the founder of Carlsberg, in 1909 and dedicated to the public in 1913. Based on a famous fairy tale by Hans Christian Andersen it depicts a mermaid sitting on a rock looking out at the shore and represents the tragic tale of a mermaid who gave up everything for the love of a prince. The statue is quite small but attracts around 1 million visitors annually.

The Little Mermaid Statue.[28]

As of the writing of this book, you can visit the Little Mermaid Statue at any time during your visit. However, please make sure to double-check the opening hours online should there be any slight changes to their schedule.

Address: Langelinie, 2100 København Ø, Denmark

The Design Museum Denmark (Designmuseum Danmark) – This museum is home to some of the most fascinating design and arts-related artifacts. The museum is in a historic treasure building in Nordre Frihavn. Once the King Frederik's hospital, the entire venue is now dedicated to Danish and international design. You will find impressive decorative arts and design exhibitions on furniture, industrial design, textiles, fashion, and more. Besides the permanent collection, the venue hosts temporary exhibitions of artifacts and interesting pieces from all over the world. The venue is home to several workshops and educational programs throughout the year.

Designmuseum Danmark.[29]

As of the writing of this book, the opening hours are Tuesday and Wednesday and Friday to Sunday from 10 am to 6 pm, Friday from 10 am to 8 pm, and closed on Monday. However, please make sure to double-check the opening hours online should there be any slight changes to their schedule.

Address: Bredgade 68, 1260 København, Denmark

TRANSPORT

S-Train – The S-Train is your best choice from Nordre Frihavn or Osterbro to other parts of the city. The reliable train system connects these neighborhoods to all parts of Copenhagen and surrounding areas. Nordhavn and the Osterport Stations are the primary hubs for the S-Train. The trains run frequently throughout the 24-hour cycle and are clean, punctual, and well-maintained.

City Buses – City buses are a great choice for traveling within the Oster-bro and Nordre Frihavn neighborhoods. An extensive bus network runs through the neighborhoods so you can get from one spot to another quickly and cost-effectively. As a tourist, focus on 1A, 3A, and 14 bus lines, which run through tourist spots, shopping areas, and dining destinations.

Cycling – As with other areas in Copenhagen, Osterbro and Nordre Frihavn are excellent for cycling. You can easily rent if you do not have your own bi-cycle and ride around the neighborhoods. There are city cycling tours, or you can enjoy scenic routes independently.

EXPERIENCES

Ostre Anlaeg Park – This large park is close to Osterbro's center. It is like a green oasis in the middle of an urban environment. The park is adjacent to the National Gallery of Denmark (SMK). You'll find lush greenery and beautiful lakes, creating a serene environment ideal for enjoying a picnic or leisurely walk. The park is home to various sculptures and art installations to enjoy as you walk through. It's excellent for birdwatching and cycling. Various seasonal events happen in the park throughout the year.

Address: Stockholmsgade 20, 2100 København, Denmark

FAMILY FUN

Faelledenparken – Faelledenparken is the largest park in Copenhagen, cov-ering over 58 hectares, and was created in 1906-1914. You will find a range of outdoor activities here, including sports facilities, playgrounds, large open green spaces, and excellent picnic spots. Multiple jogging, running, and cy-cling tracks are a great way to engage with locals and enjoy fun activities. The park is a venue for many events and festivals throughout the year, including the Copenhagen Carnival.

Address: 2200 Copenhagen, Denmark

Kastellet (The Citadel) - The Citadel in Osterbro is one of Northern Europe's most impressive military bases. It was constructed in the 17th century close to the harbor. The fortress played a major role in defending Copenhagen over the centuries and is one of the border fortresses that made it highly challenging for attackers to gain access. Today, the site is a functional military base open to the public. You can walk along the ramparts to enjoy views of the well-maintained grounds and surrounding areas. Several historic buildings and monuments are within the compound.

Kastellet (The Citadel).[30]

Address: Gl. Hovedvagt, Kastellet 1, 2100 København, Denmark

Ostre Anlaeg Park - This is another historic and beautiful park in Osterbro. This area was originally part of the city's old fortifications, but in the late 19th century, it was transformed into a public park. The area features picturesque lakes, winding paths, and lush greenery making it a fantastic option if you want to relax, go for a leisurely walk, and spend time with your loved ones. Within the park, you will also find the Statens Museum for Kunst (The National Gallery of Denmark), where you can view and enjoy world-class exhibitions.

Statens Museum for Kunst (The National Gallery of Denmark).[31]

WHERE TO EAT

Gro Spiseri – Gro Spiseri offers one of Copenhagen's most interesting dining experiences. The restaurant is on the rooftop of an urban farm in Osterbro and focuses on farm-to-table dining, with nearly all ingredients grown onsite or sourced locally. They focus on sustainability and promoting local produce. Naturally, the menu varies according to the seasons and what is available. They have an ala carte menu, so you can enjoy a communal dining experience with a multi-course meal that highlights fresh, organic produce.

The atmosphere on the rooftop provides a unique setting, letting you enjoy stunning views of the city. Gro Spiseri is an excellent choice for an intimate dinner experience.

Address: Æbeløgade 4, 2100 Østerbro, Denmark

Kiin Kiin- Kiin Kiin (come and eat) is a world-renowned Michelin-starred Thai restaurant in Osterbro. Its upscale dining experience blends traditional Thai flavors with modern cooking techniques. The tasty menu includes a modern take on classic Thai dishes, focusing on bold flavors expressed in an exquisite and singular presentation. Two famous dishes include *Tom Yum Soup* and *Crispy Duck*.

Address: Guldbergsgade 21, 2200 København, Denmark

Cafe Bopa – This charming, classic cafe offers an unusual menu, especially for breakfast, brunch, and lunch. The cafe focuses on light dishes, such as the breakfast menu and all-day snacks, including salads, sandwiches, and some brunch options. One of the best they offer is the weekend brunch menu, but you must wait for the weekend. The setting adds to the café's charm – you can sit outside and enjoy the atmosphere while enjoying your meal.

Address: Løgstørgade 8, 2100 København, Denmark

LUMSKEBUGTEN

Lumskebugten is a nice place to have dinner with friends. It serves European, Scandinavian, and Danish dishes, such as pea soup, egg and shrimp, roast beef, and spejleæg. For dessert, you can order their delicious Profitroles. The atmosphere is cozy, friendly, and relaxed. The staff and overall service are excellent. After your meal, you can enjoy taking a walk along the waterfront to enjoy the view.

Address: Esplanaden 21, Copenhagen 1263 Denmark

Ø12 – COFFEE & EATERY

Ø12 is a cozy yet stylish eatery and cafe that serves specialty coffee. It also has breakfast, lunch, and brunch dishes. Their breakfast is what people come for the most, serving classic eggs benedict, avocado toast, and soft, fluffy pancakes topped with fresh fruit you can enjoy with the fresh juices guests swear by. A great option for a hot drink after brunch is their Chai Latte. If you go at night, you can enjoy their drinks, such as fancy wine and cocktails. The place is busy, so it is better to make a reservation before you go.

Address: Øster Farimagsgade 12b, Copenhagen 2100 Denmark

PETIT CAFÉ

Petit Café is a cozy, French-style café with outdoor seating facing the street. It is the perfect place to enjoy a delicious breakfast with friends. Their breakfast dishes include multiple options of omelets. They serve baked goods and sweets, such as organic rye bread buns, croissants, pain au chocolat, cookies, and rum balls. For brunch, you can order their croque madame, chevre chaud, or salmon salad.

Address: Nordre Frihavnsgade 43, 2100 København, Denmark

Nordre Frihavnsgade – This is another top-rated shopping destination well known for its charming atmosphere and diverse range of shops. You will find a good mix of high-end, independent, and specialty stores. Whether home decor, artisanal goods, or fashion and accessories, you will find it here. The street is home to several eateries, including the best cafes in the city. The cafes, restaurants, and bakeries are great places to enjoy a snack and refuel after a hard day's shopping.

Address: 2100 Copenhagen, Denmark

Osterbrogade – Osterbrogade is one of the main shopping areas in Osterbro, and it has a wide selection of stores and retail outlets. This shopping street features high-end and mid-range fashion outlets, several department stores, and popular chain stores. It's a great place to visit as there is always something happening. You can enjoy a full day here walking through the street, soaking in the atmosphere, and enjoying the city's friendly vibe.

Address: 2100 Copenhagen, Denmark.

TorvehallerneKBH - The Torvehallerne market is just outside the Osterbro area near the Norreport Station. It is a must-visit location for food enthusiasts and is considered one of the city's best food markets. Over 60 stalls sell gourmet food products, ready-to-eat meals, fresh local produce, and various Danish specialties. You can sample plenty of international cuisines and artisanal products. The market has an outdoor and indoor seating area with a bustling atmosphere perfect for shopping and sampling foods.

The Torvehallerne market.[32]

Address: Frederiksborggade 21, 1362 København, Denmark

DEN FRIE UDSTILLINGSBYGNING (THE FREE EXHIBITION BUILDING)

This art gallery near the Ostre Anlaeg Park in Osterbro, designed by Jens Ferdinand Willumsen, is an architectural marvel. The gallery focuses on contemporary art and showcases work by Danish and international artists. Various exhibitions covering paintings, sculptures, and multimedia installations are on display. Cultural events, workshops, artist talks, and seminars are part of the bustling art scene. It is a fantastic place to visit if you are a fan of contemporary art.

Address: Oslo Pl. 1, 2100 København, Denmark

OSTRE ANLAEG PARK

This is one of the most interesting parks in the city of Copenhagen in the Osterbro area. Originally, this establishment was a military fortification that secured the old city, but later, in the 19th century, it was transformed into a public park. Today, the location is home to lakes, pathways, and amazing scenery. Within the park, you will find the Statens Museum for Kunst (the National Gallery of Denmark), where visitors can indulge in world-class art exhibitions.

ENIGMA – MUSEUM OF COMMUNICATION

The Enigma museum focuses on communication, the history of communication, and also the role of communication in today's society. In recent times the museum has pivoted its focus more towards modern communication and aims to increase awareness and understanding among the young of an increasingly digital world. In the basement, you can find an arcade area where you can enjoy games like Commodore, Playstation, Nintendo, and others. The basement is a permanent exhibition known as Arcadeum and on other floors, there are different exhibitions happening throughout the year. As the name suggests, here you can also see the oldest Enigma machine used in World War 2.

The Enigma museum.[33]

Address: Øster Allé 3, 2100 København Ø, Denmark

SPORTS AND LEISURE

Osterbro Stadium

Osterbro Stadium is one of Copenhagen's biggest and most prominent sports facilities. The stadium is a popular venue for local sports and frequently hosts football matches and athletics competitions. Osterbro Stadium is where you'll find your sports entertainment. When not used as a sports venue, the stadium's facilities are open to the public for running, jogging, and other fitness activities.

Address: Gunnar Nu Hansens Pl. 7, nr. 7, 2100 København, Denmark

Faelledparken - This is the largest park in Copenhagen, and along with massive green areas, it also offers some excellent sports facilities and leisure activities. Here, you will find multiple basketball courts, football fields, and skate parks. It's a popular sports venue for both organized sports events and casual games. The open green areas are perfect for jogging, walking, picnicking, and multiple community events.

Address: Østerbro, 2100 København, Denmark

Telia Parken

Telia Parken is the national stadium of Denmark, where the national football team plays its home games, and FC Copenhagen has its home ground. It's also a grand venue for large-scale concerts and events. Many of the large television events, sporting events, and concerts all happen at this venue. This is an all-purpose venue as it has a sliding roof and can be used year-round. Be sure to check if there is anything happening at Telia Parken when you are in Copenhagen.

Telia Parken.[34]

Address: Per Henrik Lings Allé 2, 2100 København, Denmark

SVANEMOLLE BEACH

Svanemolle Beach is a man-made beach that is a unique spot for swimming and sunbathing in Osterbro City. You can enjoy popular beach activities and water sports, including windsurfing, kayaking, paddle boarding, and beach volleyball. The best part is that the water is relatively shallow, making it suitable for children.

Address: 2100, Denmark

ACCOMMODATION

Serviced Apartments – Serviced apartments give you the best of both worlds. You can enjoy accommodation that has the comfort of your home and some services you would find in a hotel. It is an excellent option for those needing more space and don't mind self-catering facilities. Serviced apartments have fully equipped kitchens, living spaces, laundry services, and other daily amenities. It is a great option if you are on a longer stay.

Bob W Osterbro Copenhagen Address: Teglværksgade 31, 2100 København, Denmark

Adina Apartment Hotel Copenhagen Address: Amerika Pl. 7, 2100 København, Denmark

Hotels – In Osterbro and Nordre Frihavn, you will find a wide selection of hotels ranging from five-star establishments to more budget-friendly accommodations. The primary benefits are the quality of service and location. Most hotels are in prime locations with excellent views and easy access to the city's most popular places and amenities.

Scandic Norreport Address: Frederiksborggade 18, 1360 København, Denmark

Comwell Copenhagen Portside Dolce by Wyndham Address: Alexandriagade 1, 2150 København, Denmark

Vacation Rentals – Vacation rentals include Airbnb, which has many accommodation options, including houses, apartments, and condos. It is a great way to live in local neighborhoods and enjoy your trip like a local. If you choose a shared home, you will meet and interact with locals more. Home shares have flexible service agreements and are budget-friendly.

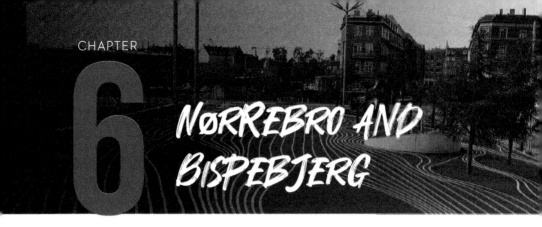

NØRREBRO AND BISPEBJERG

A BIT ABOUT NORREBRO AND BISPEBJERG

NORREBRO

Norrebro is northwest of the main city center and one of the first areas developed outside the old city's walls. This working-class area underwent heavy industrialization during the late 19th and early 20th centuries. This drastic growth attracted a diverse population of workers from other parts of the country and foreign lands. As a middle-class neighborhood, it was densely populated and faced its share of challenges.

However, the influx of immigrants brought cultural diversity. People from distant countries, including Africa, Asia, and the Middle East, enhanced the multicultural atmosphere. Unlike other parts of Copenhagen, where people from other Scandinavian countries and neighboring European countries live, Norrebro was a truly unique environment.

As the country moved from the industrial dependency, the population's needs changed, and the area underwent major evolution and development. Today, the old industrial buildings have been converted into modern housing solutions, and older establishments have been converted into cafes, restaurants, and art spaces. However, it maintains a bohemian vibe and is a creative hub for street art and nightlife. The area is a bustling environment full of new businesses and efforts to maintain its cultural heritage.

BISPEBJERG

Bispebjerg is next to Norrebro. This district in Copenhagen is one of the few areas that has been developed as a planned residential area. The development of Bispebjerg began in the early 20th century. The main focus was to provide a higher quality of living for residents escaping overcrowded inner-city districts. Bispebjerg is known for its spacious layout and plentiful green spaces with the best examples of Danish expressionist architecture, such as the Grundtvig's Church.

The area is home to a mix of private housing areas and public housing projects. Here, you will find plenty of parks, recreational areas, and facilities, making this one of Copenhagen's best family-friendly places to live. Many community-focused and community-driven projects promote social cohesion and engagement. Local festivals happen throughout the year, and several community gardens and cultural centers encourage people to come together and enhance their social life.

Over time, as Bispebjerg evolved into a modern residential area with modern amenities, it retained its charm as a spacious and healthy living environment. It is a quiet part of town, ideal for families and those wanting their home in a more tranquil environment than the busy city center.

Did You Know?

Norrebro is where people from all over the world come together. Nearly 16% of Norrebro's population does not have a Danish passport.

ASSISTENS CEMETERY

One of Copenhagen's oldest cemeteries, it was established in 1760. It is unique because not only is it a burial ground but also a beautiful park and cultural site. Moreover, several notable Danes have been laid to rest, including Hans Christian Andersen, the famous writer, and the Danish philosopher Soren Kierkegaard. You can join a guided tour showing you some of the cemetery's most notable areas, prominent graves, and cultural parts. If visiting graves is not your thing, you can always spend time in the lush green areas and enjoy a walk or a picnic in the wide-open expanse.

Assistens Cemetery.[35]

As of the writing of this book, Assistens Cemetery is open every day from 7 am to 10 pm. However, please make sure to double-check the opening hours online should there be any slight changes to their schedule.

Address: Kapelvej 2, 2200 Nørrebro, Denmark

Grundtvig's Church (Grundtvigs Kirke) – Grundtvig's Church is one of Bispebjerg's best attractions and is a visual marvel with an interesting history. The church's structure is considered one of the best examples of classic Danish architecture. Designed by architect Peder Vilhelm Jenses-Klint and completed in 1926, it is dedicated to N.F.S. Grundtvig, a renowned Danish poet, philosopher, and pastor. When visiting the church, explore the grand interior, which is as impressive, if not more so, than the exterior. Various events and concerts are held at this venue, so check out what is happening before visiting, as you may get to enjoy an event. If you have seen a Copenhagen church in photos, you can be quite confident it is the Grundtvig Church.

Grundtvig's Church.[36]

As of the writing of this book, the opening hours are:

✦ *Closed on Monday*

✦ *Tuesday from 10 am to 4 pm*

✦ *Wednesday from 1 pm to 3 pm*

✦ *Thursday from 2 pm to 4 pm*

✦ *Friday from 6 pm to 12 am*

✦ *Saturday from 10 am to 12 pm and from 2 pm to 4 pm*

✦ *Sunday from 12 pm to 4 pm.*

However, please make sure to double-check the opening hours online should there be any slight changes to their schedule.

Address: På Bjerget 14B, 2400 København NV, Denmark

BISPEBJERG HOSPITAL'S BOTANICAL GARDEN

This botanical garden on the Bispebjerg Hospital's premises is a hidden treasure, home to several plant species and beautifully landscaped gardens. It is a therapeutic space for patients, hospital staff, the public, and visitors. It's another great place to enjoy a picnic or admire the flowers in full bloom during the summer months.

As of the writing of this book, Bispebjerg Hospital's Botanical Garden is open 24 hours every day. However, please make sure to double-check the opening hours online should there be any slight changes in their schedule.

Address: Bispebjerg Bakke 23, 2400 København, Denmark

TRANSPORT

Metro (Cityringen – M3 Line) – The metro train system is one of the best ways to get around the city. For the Norrebro and Bispebjerg region, the Cityringen M3 line of the Copenhagen Metro system will be the most useful. This line has multiple stops around the Norrebro and Bispebjerg regions and offers quick and economical transport. Metro lines run frequently throughout the day and at night, so this is a 24/7 solution for travelers. Norrebro station is the central point.

Buses – Another excellent option for public transport is the local buses. For the Norrebro and Bispebjerg regions, the 5C, 6A, and 350S buses are best. These buses provide direct access to residential areas, shopping areas, and key attractions. The main benefit of buses is they access many important areas the Metro does not reach. Also, traveling by bus lets you enjoy the city's scenic beauty. A bus is ideal for shorter trips.

EXPERIENCES

Banana Park (Bananparken) – This park is one of Norrebro's hidden gems. Banana Park is a community-driven recreational space with murals, a climbing wall, and green space to play or laze on. It is frequently used for community events, performances, and workshops, so it is a great way to get a taste of Norrebro's community spirit and interact with the locals.

Address: Nannasgade 6, 2200 Kobenhavn, Denmark

FAMILY FUN

Superkilen Park – The Superkilen is a modern park in Norrebro that reflects the area's cultural diversity. Divided into three sections, the park caters to families and children. There are plenty of activities to keep the kids busy for hours and a delightful atmosphere in which parents can relax.

Superkilen Park.[37]

Address: Nørrebrogade 210, 2200 København, Denmark

The Red Square (Rode Plads) – The Red Square is a section within the Su-perkilen, and, as the name suggests, it has a red and orange color scheme. It is one of the park's most vibrant and prominent areas with a dynamic layout. You will find activities like a skate park, basketball courts, ping-pong tables, and much more. Art installations from all around the world are a fascinating aspect of the park; children and adults will have a great time exploring. For adults, there are exercise machines to try out.

Address: Nørrebrogade 210, 2200 København, Denmark

The Black Market (Den Sorte Plads) – The Black Market is a central part of the Superkilen and is more of a meeting point. This area features a darker and smoother color scheme with black and white theme colors. It is a great place for a picnic with plenty of seats and shady spots, barbecue pits, and benches in different styles and shapes. Moreover, chess tables are placed all around this area. Also, enjoy the local food market in this part of the park.

Address: 2200 Copenhagen, Denmark

Jaegersborggade Street – This street is another vibrant part of town where you can find specialty boutiques, art galleries, and vintage shops. It is the place to go for exclusive fashion items, handmade crafts, and contemporary art pieces. The street is well-known for its diverse culinary scene, where you will find cafes, bakeries, and gourmet food shops. As you walk along the street, sample organic treats, enjoy a warm beverage at the cafes, or enjoy a meal at one of the gourmet restaurants.

Address: 2200 Copenhagen, Denmark

WHERE TO EAT

Meyers Bageri – Meyers Bageri, founded by the renowned Danish chef Claus Meyer, is a well-known local establishment that offers the best bread and pas-tries in the city. The tastiest items include Kanelsnurrer (cinnamon swirl) and Rugbrod (rye bread). If you are in the neighborhood and looking for a quick snack or something small to enjoy with tea or coffee, visit Meyers Bageri for a pastry or sandwich.

Address: Jaegersborggade 9, 2200 Kobenhavn, Denmark.

La Neta – La Neta is one of the most popular eateries in the Norrebro area, offering authentic Mexican street food. So much so that they have imported their own tortilla press from Mexico and strive to source the finest local ingredients and get other traditional ingredients imported to offer the most genuine and delicious taste experience. Moreover, here you will find an excellent selection of mescal and tequila. They have recently also teamed up with Mikkeller to provide 10+ taps of the classic Mikkeller bear alongside their tasty Mexican offerings, which is just in line with the multicultural theme of Norrebro.

Address: Nørrebrogade 29, 2200 København, Denmark

Grod – Grod is a reliable, budget-friendly, high-quality eatery in Copenhagen. The restaurant has branches in many areas of the city, including Norrebro and Bispebjerg. This medium-priced restaurant is affordable even when visiting with a large group or family. The restaurant specializes in local comfort foods, especially porridge. You can add different toppings and flavors to take the meal to the next level. Some of the best meals include barley risotto with mushrooms and parmesan and classic oatmeal with caramel sauce and apple compote.

Address: kl tv, Jægersborggade 50, 2200 København, Denmark

OYSTERS AND GRILL

Oysters and Grill is a casual seafood and barbecue restaurant popular for its festive foods, such as shelled prawns, clams, langoustines, squid ceviche, steak tartare, and rib-eye. It is perfect for dinner, a late-night snack, or drinks. The staff is pleasant, professional, and happy to help. They offer both set menus and a la carte, with gluten-free options, if preferred. Making a reservation is better to ensure a table.

Address: Sjællandsgade 1B, Copenhagen 2200 Denmark

HOOKED CARLSBERG BYEN

Hooked Carlsberg Byen is one the best seafood restaurants in Copenhagen, with an industrial and modern design. From their crunchy fish burger, delicate fries, tasty truffle mayo, poke bowls, especially the salmon, mac and cheese croquettes, and halloumi burger, it is guaranteed to make you come back for more. If you are an Asian food lover, their Asian lobster roll and vinegar fries with truffle mayo is a must-try. It is a lovely place to spend a sunny evening with friends or family.

Address: Købkes Pl. 36, Copenhagen 1770 Denmark

SASAA

Sasaa is an African cuisine restaurant with options for vegan and vegetarian dishes. If you like spicy food, this restaurant is for you. When they say spicy, they really mean it. It is not for the faint of heart. The interior is cozy with paintings of African people on the walls. The menu includes fried cassava, fried plantain, jollof, chicken peanut butter stew, and drinks like ginger beer and hibiscus. The service is fast and friendly, and the restaurant is clean with warm lighting.

Address: Blaagaardsgade 2A, Copenhagen 2200 Denmark

SHOPPING GUIDE

Jaeggersbrogade – This is one of the most famous streets in Norrebro, well-known for shopping and leisure. It is a fantastic mix of cafes and shops alongside some exciting art galleries. In the past, this used to be a middle-class neighborhood, but today, it has evolved to become a cultural hub. In terms of shopping options, you can find high-end boutique stores, international brands, and other well-known outlets. Also, you will find a number of vintage stores, handmade jewelry stores, and places selling specialty coffee and other local goods. When in Jaeggerbrogade, be sure to visit *Karamelleriet*, which is a local candy store offering handmade sweets.

Address: 2200 Copenhagen, Denmark

Packyard – Packyard operates out of 22 Elmegde and was brought to life by the two founders Nikolaj and Anders. The object with Packyard was to offer an urban outdoor men's fashion outlet with a touch of Norrebro fashion. In recent years the urban outdoor niche has grown in popularity as people enjoy the utilitarian yet comfortable and also trendy look. Packyard brings together several brands in this niche together so you can get a complete urban outdoor solution under one roof. Here, you will always find something new, some new brand or some new article. Have a look at their website to see what it's all about.

Address: Elmegade 22, 2200 København, Denmark

Superkilen Market – This market is located within the Superkilen park. A wide range of products from local vendors, including fresh produce, handmade crafts, and food and drinks, are available in this market. The focus is on local shopping and culture, so this is a good market to explore for unique souvenirs, handicrafts, and traditional Danish products. You will find local artisans selling their products, and it's a great place to try Danish food from the many food stalls. There is an international food stall section for you to explore.

Assistens Kirkegard Flea Market – This flea market is by the Assistens Cemetery. It is a fantastic place to find products at budget prices. For things typically hard to find, such as vintage goods, antiques, classic books, and second-hand treasures, this is a market you will thoroughly enjoy. The main stalls include vintage clothing, local crafts, and antique shops.

ENTERTAINMENT

Norrebrogade - If you want entertainment, you don't need to look much further than Norrebrogade Street. This popular area is home to a range of activities and buzzes with an exciting and vibrant energy no matter when you visit. On either side of the street are bars, restaurants, cafes, and plenty of outlets offering nightlife, socialization, and entertainment. This street encapsulates the diverse cultural landscape that is Norrebro's hallmark. It's a fantastic place to hang out and enjoy.

Address: 2200 Copenhagen, Denmark

Blagards Plads – This is another historic area of Norrebro that is still extremely popular today. This square is in Norrebro central and is well-known for its cultural and artistic significance. A range of events occur throughout the year, including outdoor concerts, festivals, and markets. Bars and cafes are plentiful where you can relax and enjoy yourself.

Address: 2200 Copenhagen, Denmark

SPORTS AND LEISURE

Bispebjerg Cemetery – While primarily established as a cemetery, the work done on the grounds, green areas, lanes, and walkways make it a lovely place for relaxation and leisure. Cherry Blossom Avenue is an exceptionally breathtaking sight when the plants are in full bloom during the spring season. It is a great place to escape from the busy and sometimes loud city life and enjoy a natural environment surrounded by natural beauty.

Address: Frederiksborgvej 125, 2400 København, Denmark

Norrebroparken - Norrebroparken is a large public park in Norrebro that is ideal for outdoor sports and leisure activities. The city has provided sports facilities, including football, basketball, and skateboarding grounds with open areas for picnics and relaxation. Whether you want a space to relax with your family or a spot to enjoy some fun-fueled activities with friends, this park is a great choice.

Address: Stefansgade 28-30, 2200 København, Denmark

ACCOMMODATION

Boutique Hotels – Boutique hotels in Norrebro and Bispebjerg offer the best accommodation options. Your choice ranges from top-of-the-line services with the best views of the district's best locations. For maximum comfort, this is the option to explore.

Hotel M18 Address: Meinungsgade 18, 2200 København, Denmark

Numa Copenhagen Norrebro Address: Drejervej 4, 2400 København, Denmark

Hostels – A hostel is ideal for budget accommodation. Depending on how many services and amenities are included, the prices will vary. Moreover, hostels allow you to interact and socialize with fellow travelers.

A&O Hostel Address: Tagensvej 135, 137, 2200 København N, Denmark

Urban Camper Hostel & Bar Address: Lygten 2C, 2400 København, Denmark

Apartment Rentals – A short-term apartment rental is a great choice for homey comfort and flexibility. You have multiple options in this category, from simple studio apartments to multi-room luxurious apartments.

CHAPTER

7

AMAGER EAST AND AMAGER WEST

A BIT ABOUT AMAGER EAST AND AMAGER WEST

AMAGER EAST

The island of Amager is east of Copenhagen, and the northern part forms part of Copenhagen. Amager East is on the island's eastern side and is closest to central Copenhagen. This area is best known for its recreational facilities, comfortable residential neighborhoods, and modern infrastructure. It is a nice mix of urban living, easy access to nature, and a beautiful beachfront.

Amager East.[38]

The Amager region's development started in the 16th century when King Christian II invited farmers to establish an agricultural area. Until the late 19th century, it was primarily used for agriculture. At the turn of the 20th century, it became more urbanized as industry developed. At the same time, residential areas expanded to accommodate the growing population. Recently, the region underwent another development phase, creating Amager Strandpark and several residential buildings, shopping areas, and recreational facilities. Today, it is a vibrant and desirable area in Copenhagen.

AMAGER WEST

As the name implies, this part of Amager is on the island's west side. This area is close to the University of Copenhagen's Amager campus and is known for its modern architecture, including sharp and striking design features. The region has excellent urban planning in which green spaces are carefully included between dense developments. It is a beautiful blend of urban convenience and natural beauty.

Like the Eastern part of Amager, this area was previously agricultural land. This part of Amager saw more development after the 20th-century war era. Development was planned and carried out strategically to make it a part of Copenhagen. One of the main developments was the Orestad area in the late 1990s, which changed the area into a modern urban district of residential, commercial, and cultural spaces. Today, this is one of Copenhagen's best residential areas.

Did You Know?

Some parts of Amager were previously (as recently as the 20th century) used as dumping grounds for sewage waste from Copenhagen city. However, the city went through a radical transformation and has evolved from an otherwise neglected part of the city to a main attraction. An example of this transformation is the development of Amager Strandpark in 2005, which consists of a 2.5 km artificial beach that is a popular tourist attraction today.

THE BLUE PLANET (DEN BLA PLANET)

The Blue Planet is North Europe's largest aquarium. The aquarium has an astonishing variety of aquatic life, from species indigenous to the Scandinavian region to aquatic animals around the globe. The aquarium is an architectural marvel designed to resemble a swirling whirlpool. The aquarium's most popular marine environments include the Ocean Tank, rainforest, and cold water exhibits. You'll find sharks, rays, sea otters, and thousands of other animals. It is a fantastic place to spend the day and a must-visit for people interested in aquatic life.

The Blue Planet (Den Bla Planet).[39]

As of the writing of this book, the opening hours are Tuesday to Sunday from 10 am to 5 pm and Monday from 10 am to 9 pm. However, please make sure to double-check the opening hours online should there be any slight changes to their schedule.

Address: Jacob Fortlingsvej 1, 2770 Kastrup, Denmark

AMAGER FAELLED

The Amager Faelled is a massive nature reserve in the heart of Amager. The diverse landscape it covers sets this reserve apart from others. The varying geography, including wetlands, forests, and meadows, is home to a variety of wildlife and is a great place to relax and unwind. The well-developed area has an excellent network of cycling and walking paths, ideal for outdoor activities, walks, sports, and birdwatching. Guided tours of the reserve are on offer.

As of the writing of this book, Amager Faelled is open 24 hours every day. However, please make sure to double-check the opening hours online should there be any slight changes to their schedule.

Address: Artillerivej 73B, 2300 Kobenhavn, Denmark

ORESTAD

Orestad, a vibrant part of Amager, features interesting architecture and is a prime example of Copenhagen's top-tier urban planning. The area mixes residential and commercial spaces interspersed with cultural venues. There is always something entertaining happening in Orestad. Key attractions in Orestad include *8 House* and *Bella Sky Hotel*, known for their architecture and unique locations. Field's shopping center is one of the biggest shopping malls in Scandinavia. Visit the Orestad Bypark and the Kalvebod Faelled nature reserve for a more natural setting.

8 House.[40]

Address: 2300, Copenhagen, Denmark

TRANSPORT

Metro - The metro is a quick and efficient way to get around Amager. The M1 and M2 main lines provide convenient access to Amager's main areas. Amagerbro, Lergavsparken, and Oresund are Amager's main metro stations. The metro reaches the city center and nearly all major attractions in the district.

Harbor Buses - The harbor bus is an exceptional, enjoyable, and scenic way to travel around Copenhagen. Since Amager has access to water on all sides, this is a great way to explore the town. The harbor bus stops at several places throughout Amager. The main stops include the islands of Brygge and Kastrup. You get a different perspective of the city and enjoy spectacular sea views from the harbor bus. The harbor bus is a great choice for sightseeing.

Buses - The bus network is as excellent in Amager as in other parts of Copenhagen. The main bus routes in the Amager district include 5C, 33, and 250S. These routes will take you to the city's main attractions and transport hubs. These routes also reach residential areas in the district. The bus is the most cost-effective mode of transport.

EXPERIENCES

DR Byen (DR City) - DR Byen is in the Orestad area and is the headquarters of the Danish Broadcasting Corporation (DR). This major cultural hub features a famous concert hall (the DR Concert Hall) designed by French architect Jean Nouvel. Visitors can take guided tours of the concert hall, considered one of the world's most beautiful and acoustically advanced concert halls. It is the venue for many of Europe's best concerts and musical performances. DR Byen is a fantastic place for anyone interested in mu-

DR Byen.[41]

sic, architecture, or media. It's a unique opportunity to explore how one of the best broadcasting companies in the world operates.

Address: Emil Holms Kanal 20, 0999 København K, Denmark

Kastrup Sobad (Kastrup Sea Bath) – Kastrup Sobad is locally referred to as 'The Snail' due to its spiral-shaped design. This bath is at the northern section of Amager Beach Park. You can swim in the Oresund waters while enjoying the bath's stunning architecture. The water is cool and extremely clean. Wooden decks and places for sunbathing surround the bath, with panoramic views of the sea and the Copenhagen skyline. This bath is open all year round and offers a plethora of additional facilities.

Kastrup Sobad (Kastrup Sea Bath).[42]

Address: Amager Strandvej 301, 2770 Kastrup, Denmark

Kalvebod Faelled – Kalvebod Faelled is another extensive nature reserve in Copenhagen in the western part of Amager. This reserve covers an impressive area of 20 square kilometers (roughly 8 square miles), including a variety of terrains, forests, meadows, and wetlands. There are several outdoor activities to enjoy- birdwatching, hiking, and cycling. The biome is home to foxes and deer and is a bird lovers' paradise with its variety, including indigenous species and migratory birds.

Copenhagen Surf School – If you are visiting in the summer time then the Copenhagen Surf School offers classes from May through September in which you can master windsurfing in just 2.5 hours. The shallow waters near Amager and the sand seabed make this an ideal place for beginners to try out surfing. The waves are calm, the water is clear the summer weather is perfect for surfing. Among the instructors are some of the best surfers from Denmark. After a quick introduction to the equipment and a briefing about how to operate it, you will be on your way to surfing. There is also a nice surfing café located close by where you can enjoy some snacks and drinks and views of the water.

Copenhagen Local Walks – Amager is the most densely populated area in Denmark, and Copenhagen Local Walks is a great way to explore each nook and cranny. Through the walking tour of the city, you will get to see chemical factories, heavy industry areas, recreational harbor parks, and award-winning architecture. Experience the neighborhood where locals refer to themselves as *Amagericans,* not *Copenhageners.* It is a unique experience for children and adults alike.

FAMILY FUN

Amager Strandpark – Amager Strandpark is one of the best beach parks in the Amager area, offering various activities for people of all ages. You can enjoy swimming in the clear water and enjoy several water sports and beach activities. The most popular activities include kayaking and windsurfing. There are multiple playgrounds, picnic areas, and barbecue spots to enjoy outdoors with friends and family. A lagoon provides a safe and calm environment where children can enjoy swimming.

Address: Amager Strand Promenaden 1, 2300 København, Denmark

Naturcenter Amager is an education nature center in the Kalvebod Faelled nature reserve. The center arranges family-friendly activities, such as guided nature walks, educational workshops about local wildlife, and birdwatching events. It's an excellent place for kids to learn about the natural environment and how we can live with nature peacefully. It is a great place to visit, relax, learn, and engage with the natural environment.

Address: Granatvej 5, 2770 Kastrup, Denmark

Copenhagen Cable Park – This cable park is in the heart of Amager and offers exciting activities for kids and adults. Here, you get to enjoy water skiing, kneeboarding, and wakeboarding. If you are new to these activities, you can rent equipment and get beginner lessons. There are different facilities for different skill levels, so there is something for everyone here.

Address: Kraftværksvej 24, 2300 København, Denmark

Urban Ranger Camp – This is a popular adventure park in Refshaleoen. The park offers activities like zip lining, wall climbing, and high-rope courses. The park is for people of all ages, so you can enjoy activities at various difficulty levels. There are dedicated activities for children and more advanced courses for adults. This park is a great way for families to spend time together, promoting communication, teamwork, and active fun.

Address: Refshalevej 177, 1432 København, Denmark

WHERE TO EAT

Restaurant Kadeau – For a fine dining experience, this restaurant is the place to go. Restaurant Kadeau offers a Michelin-star dining experience and specializes in New Nordic Cuisine. The team finds artful and unique ways to present seasonal and locally sourced ingredients that please all the senses. The chef's tasting menu is the best option, giving you a taste of everything. The main things to look forward to are the grilled scallops with wild herbs and the wine-pairing experience.

Address: Wildersgade 10B, 1408 København, Denmark

H3 Amager Fiskehus – This is both an old and a new establishment. In the past, it was known just as Amager Fiskehus (fishmonger) and was a place where people came by to get their hands on the fresh catch of the day. Amager Fiskehus has been in business since the late 19th century and continues to date. However, the fifth-generation owners Rikke and Lars have opened up a small restaurant with just 28 seats right next to the shop. Here, you can enjoy a wide variety of seafood served in the classic and authentic Danish way.

Address: Holmbladsgade 3, 2300 København, Denmark

Wulff and Konstali – Wulff and Konstali is a local eatery that is well-known for its breakfast and brunch menu. The food is beautifully presented, and the flavors are top-notch. The best dish is the brunch board. You can select five or seven items from the extensive menu for the board or platter. The best items for your board should include chia pudding, freshly baked pastries, and avocado toast. Their coffee comes highly recommended.

Address: Lergravsvej 57, 2300 København, Denmark

Il Buco – Part of the charm of Il Buco is the atmosphere. The restaurant nestles beside the canal, offering spectacular city views, and is especially enjoyable at night. The restaurant offers Italian cuisine, including classics such as wood-fired pizzas and homemade pasta dishes. This restaurant is fabulous for enjoying incredible views and delicious food without breaking the bank.

Address: Njalsgade 19C, 2300 København, Denmark

POMODORO D'ORO

Pomodoro D'Oro is an Italian restaurant located in the Østerbro and Amager areas. It is a pizzeria known for its authentic pizza and pasta dishes made from handpicked, fresh, and organic ingredients. The menu has gourmet dishes, including vegetarian and vegan options. It is a beautifully decorated place with both indoor and outdoor seating options. Whether you are looking to enjoy a romantic date night, late-night drinks, or a place for business meetings, Pomodoro D'Oro is a choice you won't regret.

Address: Amager Strandvej 130A, 2300 København, Denmark

ALCHEMIST

Alchemist is a Michelin-star restaurant founded by chef Rasmus Munk in 2015. This fine dining restaurant with two Michelin stars is among the top 50 restaurants in the world. The food presentation is unique; you will never find anything like it anywhere, such as the shape of the human eye, heads, and tiny human hearts and brains. The interiors blend elements of nature and art. The walls are decorated with bold, colorful installations by Lady AIKO, a graffiti artist who captures the multicultural energy of New York in her artwork. The restaurant also displays a light and sound show of LED lights that reflect the challenges of the LGBTQ+ community.

Address: Refshalevej 173C, 1432 København K, Denmark

FUSION

Fusion is a great restaurant to enjoy a nice brunch with friends. The atmosphere is lovely, and the staff is very pleasant and friendly. They are known for their big portions. They have pork burgers, spicy tuna, chicken bao, and fried chicken curry that you cannot miss! People also recommend their fried noodles with chicken. It is the perfect place to go after a long day. After your meal, you can enjoy a brisk walk in the dog park nearby.

Address: Amager Strandvej 22L, 2300 København, Denmark

SHOPPING GUIDE

Field's Shopping Center – The Fields shopping center is one of Denmark's biggest shopping centers, offering a wide variety of stores. You will find everything from high-end fashion brands to retail chains, home decor, food and beverages, electronics, superb dining, and more.

Address: Arne Jacobsens Allé 12, 2300 København, Denmark

Amager Centret – This is another popular shopping center in the heart of Amager. It is much smaller than Fields Shopping Center. However, it has a great variety of stores. Although this shopping center focuses on local Danish brands and is a great spot for everyday shopping, it has stores from several industries, so it is a complete shopping solution under one roof. Also, it has an excellent food court with a plethora of dining options.

Address: Reberbanegade 3, 2300 Amager Øst, Denmark

Amagerbrogade – This popular street is known for shopping. On either side of the street are wide selections of shops offering everything from high-end goods, boutique outlets, mid-tier stores, local Danish chains, several unique stores, second-hand stores, and specialty stores offering handmade goods. The lively street atmosphere sets this location apart from others.

Address: 2300 Copenhagen, Denmark

Nordic Nesting – This specialty boutique focuses on products made with Scandinavian design elements. You will find everything from furniture to home decor to lifestyle products. It is a fantastic place to pick up a souvenir that is truly Danish. Enjoy browsing lighting options, accessories, ceramics, textiles, and decorative products. Scandinavian design focuses on clean lines and minimalist aesthetics, so finding something that suits your taste and needs with in-store shopping assistance will be easy.

Address: Terminalgade, 2770 Kastrup, Denmark

ENTERTAINMENT

Prags Boulevard – This is a colorful and lively part of Amager, known for its vibrant street art, spacious green areas, and publicly available recreational facilities. It is an ideal place for families, especially those with younger children. It has several playgrounds, sports facilities, and picnic areas. This venue often hosts events, markets, and outdoor festivals, so it's a great place to catch up with local family-friendly entertainment.

Address: 2300 Copenhagen, Denmark

Refshaleoen – Refshaleoen was a purely industrial area in the past. However, it has been restructured and evolved into a cultural and entertainment hub. It has several venues where you can find a diverse crowd and multiple forms of entertainment. The most popular attractions include street food markets, local art galleries, and water sports activities near the harbor. Events and concerts happen here from time to time, including one of Copenhagen's most famous art galleries, *The Copenhagen Contemporary*, renowned for large-scale installations and exhibitions.

Address: 1432 Copenhagen Municipality, Denmark

DR Koncerthuset (DR Concert Hall) – The DR Concert Hall is in the DR Byen area and is one of the city's best entertainment venues. Designed by Jean Nouvel, it hosts premium musical performances from various genres, including rock concerts, classical music, jazz, and family shows.

Address: Ørestads Blvd. 13, 2300 København, Denmark

Amager Bio – Amager Bio is a popular local concert hall. Previously, this used to be a cinema which is why it offers some of the best acoustics of any venue in the city. Also, because it was a cinema, it is much smaller and offers a more intimate experience than bigger venues. The venue has hosted musicians and performances from a broad variety of genres, including opera, rock, classical, and more. Also, here you can see performances, films, and Marionette Theater. Definitely worth looking into if you are in the Amager area.

SPORTS AND LEISURE

Amager Common (Amager Faelled) – This large nature reserve in Amager offers expansive green spaces, diverse wildlife, and a fantastic outdoor environment for activities. The reserve has several walking and cycling trails that are ideal for a casual stroll and more intense exercise. Multiple picnic spots are scattered around the reserve where you can immerse yourself in the beautiful natural environment.

Islands Brygge Harbor Bath – This is a unique swimming spot in the city center where you can enjoy open-air swimming just next to the harbor in a controlled environment. Here, you will find 5 pools designed for people of different ages. Two of these are dedicated to children, with the shallowest pool for children being just 30cm deep. There are also different diving boards available, which are one meter, three meters, and five meters high, respectively. You get a fantastic view of the city skyline as you swim. Here you will commonly see people swimming in the summer days after work on their way home. The quality of water is pristine as it is checked daily, and swimmers are only allowed in if authorities deem it fit for swimming.

Islands Brygge Harbor Bath.[43]

Address: Islands Brygge 14, 2300 København S, Denmark

Royal Golf Center – This is one of the city's best golfing centers in Orestad. It is an 18-hole championship course with a smaller 9-hole short course. The driving range and practice facilities are excellent, and the clubhouse features several dining options.

Address: Center Blvd. 4, 2300 Copenhagen S, Denmark

ACCOMMODATION

Hostels and Guesthouses – Backpacker hostels are the most economical accommodation option. However, these are best for singles, as communal rooms often accommodate 5-10 people. Some hostels provide private rooms. Guesthouses are another convenient and budget-friendly choice, especially if you need space for kids or want to stay in a single room as a couple.

Urban House Copenhagen Address: Colbjørnsensgade 5,.11, 1652 København, Denmark

Copenhagen Backpackers Hostel Address: Reventlowsgade 10A, 1651 København, Denmark

Hotels – Amager has an excellent selection of hotels throughout the district. The best hotels command the best locations, often with main attractions within walking distance.

Another option is a hotel near the waterfront with an excellent view of the Norrebro and the beach. Also, some 3-star hotels offer an excellent experience at more affordable prices.

Hotel Amager Address: Amagerbrogade 29, 2300 København, Denmark

Crowne Plaza Copenhagen Towers, an IHG Hotel Address: Copenhagen Towers, Ørestads Blvd. 114, 118, 2300 København, Denmark

Apartments – If you plan on staying a while or want accommodation with a bit more flexibility, then an apartment is ideal. Moreover, apartments allow you to live where you want and are available in all Amager's areas. Apartments are best for larger groups and families.

8

BRONSHOJ-HUSUM AND VANLOSE

A BIT ABOUT BRONSHOJ-HUSUM AND VANLOSE

BRONSHOJ-HUSUM

The first recorded mention of Bronshoj is in 1186. The area is one of Copenhagen's oldest parts. Initially, it was a small village settlement. Husum was a rural village located to the northwest of Bronshoj. Later, the area developed into a residential suburb as Copenhagen grew in the 19th and 20th centuries. The town of Husum became urbanized in the 20th century.

Bronshoj Church.[44]

VANLOSE

Vanlose's history is like Bronshoj, a small rural village dating back to the 13th century. Like Bronshoj, the area underwent a major phase of urbanization and development in the 19th century and evolved into a suburb. The development of the railway network was significant in Copenhagen's expansion and establishing the area as residential. The Vanlose station opened in 1898 and marked a milestone in the area's development and transformation. Today, Vanlose is well-known as a quality residential neighborhood in Copenhagen.

MAIN ATTRACTIONS

DAMHUSSØEN AND DAMHUSENGEN

These are two interconnected large open spaces that offer a natural environment for people to relax in the middle of the city's hustle and bustle. Damhussoen is a large lake, and Damhusengen is a park adjacent to the lake. They are ideal for picnics, outdoor activities, and family fun, especially in the warmer summer months.

As of the writing of this book, Damhussoen and Damhusengen are open 24 hours every day. However, please make sure to double-check the opening hours online should there be any slight changes to their schedule.

Address: Vanlose, Copenhagen, Denmark

UTTERSLEV MOSE

For nature-lovers, the Utterslev Mose reserve is a must-see. One of the city's largest nature reserves, it comprises multiple lakes and wetlands, home to a wide variety of birds and animal life. The has numerous hiking trails of differing endurance levels.

As of the writing of this book, Utterslev Mose is open 24 hours every day. However, please make sure to double-check the opening hours online should there be any slight changes to their schedule.

Utterslev Mose reserve.[45]

Address: Mosesvinget, 2400 Kobenhavn NV, Denmark

BRONSHOJ WATER TOWER

A historic water tower built in 1928, it was a milestone in urban planning and development as it allowed nearby households to get pressurized water straight from their taps. Today, the water tank is no longer operational but is a popular venue for events and exhibitions. It's a great way to see how far urban development has come and also how far Copenhagen has come from its humble beginnings.

Address: Brønshøjvej 29, 2700 København, Denmark

Bronshoj Water Tower.[46]

VANLOSE KULTUR STATION

This arena is the main cultural center in Vanlose and is often the venue of choice for concerts, theater performances, and artistic workshops. Moreover, there is a sizeable local culture and arts section where you can view work from local artists and artisans. If you are in the Vanlose area and want to attend a community event, check out the Vanlose Kultur Station. There is usually always something happening in this vibey arts arena.

As of the writing of this book, Vanlose Kultur Station is open every day from 8 am to 8 pm. However, please make sure to double-check the opening hours online should there be any slight changes to their schedule.

Address: Kulturhus og borgerservice, Frode Jakobsens plads 4, 1. sal Bibliotek, Jernbane Allé 38, 2720 København, Denmark

GRONDALSPARKEN

This large park in Copenhagen stretches across multiple districts, including Vanlose. The park features walking and cycling tracks, playgrounds, and dedicated sports facilities. It's a great place to work out or relax and unwind with friends and family. There are picnic spots and play areas for adults and children.

As of the writing of this book, the park is open 24 hours every day. However, please make sure to double-check the opening hours online should there be any slight changes to their schedule.

Address: Copenhagen, Denmark

TRANSPORT

S-Tog – The S-Tog is a specialized suburban rail system connecting various districts in Copenhagen, including the Bronshoj and Vanlose areas. For the Vanlose area, The main S-Tog line in Vanlose is the *F Line*. This line will connect you to many parts of Vanlose and Bronshoj and other parts of Copenhagen. If you are traveling long distances within the city, this is a great option.

Metro – Another quick and efficient railway solution is the metro. Use the *M1* and *M2* lines, which run from the Vanlose Station. The metro is an excellent option as the trains are frequent, the service is quick, and the metro reaches the city center and many main tourist attractions.

Buses – Several bus lines serve the Bronshoj and Vanlose areas. You need to look for the 2A, 5C, and 6A lines. If traveling to locations within the Bronshoj and Vanlose districts, the bus is your best option, as the routes run deep into residential areas. Train lines mostly stick to commercial and tourist areas.

Cycling – Bronshoj and Vanlose districts are well-equipped with bike lanes and bike-sharing stations, making renting a bicycle and exploring easy. It is often the best way to explore the area as you can look at things at your own pace and uncover places you would otherwise overlook when traveling on public or private transport.

EXPERIENCES

Mosen (Peblinge Lake) – Peblinge Lake, locally known as *Mosen*, is a beautiful waterfront location within the city. It has fabulous walking, jogging, and cycling tracks surrounding the lake. It's an ideal spot for families to spend quality time together, picnic near the water, or enjoy birdwatching.

Vanlose Kulturhus – This is a well-known cultural center in Vanlose which hosts a variety of events, concerts, theater performances, community activities, and art exhibitions throughout the year. You can also enjoy live music performances, participate in workshops, and explore local art exhibitions. If you are in Vanlose, it is worth checking for upcoming events at the Vanlose Kulturhus.

FAMILY FUN

Utterslev Mose – Utterslev Mose is a large nature reserve featuring a wetland area and offers an outdoor experience for people of all ages. You can enjoy walking and cycling tracks, birdwatching activities, and picnicking here. Moreover, there are also some designated areas for fishing and multiple options to explore the rich biodiversity. It's a great spot for a day out in nature to learn about wildlife while having fun. The reserve has multiple onsite amenities where you can enjoy food and also get rental equipment for the onsite activities.

Traktorstedet Vestamager – The Traktorstedet Vestamager offers a unique experience that people of all ages will enjoy. It is located right at the edge of Kalvebod Faelled Nature Reserve, and from the patio, you get to see an uninterrupted view of over 2000 hectares of pure nature reserve. The best bit is there is a café serving up some delicious food for you to enjoy while you soak in the view. This facility is open year-round and depending on which season you visit, you will get a unique view to enjoy. It's not unusual for people to see wild animals, especially deer, while they are out on the patio enjoying their meal or drinks. You can also rent outdoor gear here if you feel like exploring the outdoors; there are bike rentals and guided nature tours. There is also a nature school where young visitors can learn more about the place.

Bellahoj Aqua Center - The Bellahoj Aqua Center is a modern swimming facility with waterpark features. It has several pools for children and adults of different skill levels. Moreover, there are diving boards and water slides you can enjoy. Health and fitness facilities offer swimming classes and water-based fitness activities. It's a great spot to enjoy water activities in a relaxed environment.

Address: Bellahojvej 1, 2700 Vanlose, Denmark

Klatreskoven – This is a popular adventure park in Vanlose that offers a range of climbing activities for people of varying skill levels and ages. The most popular activities include climbing courses, zip lines, and rope bridges. Whether you are a beginner or an advanced climber, there are facilities to suit your needs.

Address: Stadionvej 80, 2600 Glostrup, Denmark

WHERE TO EAT

Taverna Kreta – Taverna Kreta is a cozy Mediterranean restaurant specializing in Greek food. The establishment offers a friendly and relaxed atmosphere, serving authentic Greek classics. The best dishes include souvlaki and moussaka, and their fresh seafood selection (octopus and calamari are very popular). It's a great place for lunch and dinner.

Address: Jagtvej 59, 2200 København, Denmark

Restaurant Kreta III – This midrange restaurant offers Greek cuisine. The best dishes include seafood platters and souvlaki. The menu offers a wide range of tastes and is an excellent option for dining with a group. The prices are reasonable, and the quality is top-notch.

Address: Jyllingevej 56, 2720 København, Denmark

Cafe Langebro – This modern and stylish cafe offers a relaxed and stylish setting. It's best known for its brunch menu and snack items. The best options include the brunch platter, gourmet burgers, and pastries. It's a great place for a casual meal or a midday snack.

Address: Islands Brygge 1B, 2300 København, Denmark

Madhjornet – This establishment focuses on Danish and Indian cuisine with a sophisticated dining environment. From the morning until 3 pm, you can enjoy classic Danish sandwiches, and then from 4 pm to 9 pm, they serve authentic Indian cuisine.

Address: Ålekistevej 143, 2720 København, Denmark

Bronshoj Bistro – Bronshoj Bistro is a kid-friendly local café and restaurant that serves Danish-style lunch dishes and homemade cakes for dessert. The restaurant also offers international, contemporary, and European dishes at reasonable prices. They also serve healthy options, if preferred. There is street parking, highchairs available, and digital payments. The service is pleasant and friendly, which makes it highly recommended by visitors.

Address: Bronshojgardsvej 1, Copenhagen 2700 Denmark

RISTORANTE LA BUCA DEGLI ARTISTI

Ristorante La Buca degli Artisti is an Italian fancy dinner restaurant where many celebrities come to eat. It has a homey, cozy atmosphere while maintaining a chic interior with white, elegant table sheets on the tables. It has glass windows to enjoy the view of people passing by on the street. The walls are decorated with pictures of famous people, such as movie stars and singers. Their cuisine includes Italian, Mediterranean, and European dishes. The wine is excellent, and for dessert, you can enjoy their pistachio ice cream served with chocolate sauce and strawberries.

Address: Godthaabsvej 209 2720 Vanlose, Copenhagen 2720 Denmark

ARMANDO'S VANLØSE

Armando's Vanløse has the best pizza in town. It is a pizza restaurant that also serves pasta dishes and sandwiches at reasonable prices. Their top pasta dish is made with beef and truffle sauce that you can't miss. The atmosphere is great, and the service is top-tier. Armando's Vanløse is where you will learn that cooking with fresh, simple, uncomplicated ingredients makes the best flavors.

Address: Jyllingevej 32, 2720 København, Denmark

SHOPPING GUIDE

Bronshoj Torv – This local market in the Bronshoj area, offering a variety of goods and services, is vibrant. Local farmers sell seasonal fruits and vegetables, artisanal products, home goods, and jewelry, and several food stalls offer snack options to keep you fueled during shopping. It's a fantastic place to purchase high-quality local produce and interact with friendly vendors in a lively atmosphere.

Address: 2700 Copenhagen, Denmark

Vanlose Torv – Vanlose Torv is a popular shopping area with a mix of shops and market stalls, including clothing, home goods, bakeries, gourmet food stores, and specialty shops. This market offers a diverse shopping experience and is as much a shopping experience as it is cultural.

Address: 2720 Copenhagen, Denmark

Spinderiet Shopping Center – This modern shopping center in Vanlose has a range of goods and services, including a wide range of high and mid-range stores with everything from fashion and clothing to electronics and home goods. The mall has a food court with restaurants and cafes ideal for a meal or a coffee break. This mall is a great place to visit for a one-stop solution for all your shopping needs.

Address: Bomuldsgade 4, 2500 København, Denmark

ENTERTAINMENT

Vanlose Culture House (Kulturstationen Vanlose) – This is a vibrant cultural center in Vanlose that hosts a number of cultural and entertainment events throughout the year. It regularly features children's theater, puppet shows, and family-friendly concerts. Creative workshops cover arts, crafts, dance, and music lessons. There are different workshops and classes for children and adults. It is a great location to enjoy some cultural and artistic experiences with your friends and family and take part in creative activities.

Grondal Multicenter – One of Copenhagen's largest sports and recreation centers, Grondal Multicenter offers several activities for all age groups. It features a fully furnished sports center with swimming pools, tennis courts, gymnasiums, multiple play areas, including indoor and outdoor play areas for children, and event spaces for tournaments. It is a fabulous recreation center for the whole family.

Address: Hvidkildevej 64, 2400 Vanløse, Denmark

Bellahoj Swimming Pool – The Bellahoj Swimming Pool Center is a fantastic recreational facility known for its high-quality amenities and a family-friendly environment. There are a number of swimming pools, including a children's pool, a leisure pool, and a lap pool. There is also a water slide and play area for children. There is also a sauna and wellness center where parents can relax and unwind while the children enjoy.

EXPERIENCE

Orestad – Orestad is located on the island of Amager and is a place known for beautiful modern architecture. Experience Orestad is a company specializing in guided architecture tours of the various establishments in the Orestad area. Some of the main buildings to look out for include the VM Houses, 8 Tallet, Tietgen Dormitory, and DR Concert Hall.

VM Houses.[47]

Norrebro Park – This park is on the border between Norrebro and Bronshoj and is easily accessible from the Bronshoj area. This is a big natural park offering green spaces and numerous activities. There are well-equipped playgrounds suitable for children of all ages and some excellent sports facilities, including football fields, basketball courts, and areas for skateboarding. The large green spaces are an excellent space for family picnics and outdoor games.

SPORTS AND LEISURE

Grondal Centret - The Grondal Centret (Multicenter) is a comprehensive sports and recreation facility offering a wide variety of activities for people of all ages. For adults, there is a gymnasium, multiple tennis courts, badminton courts, and a dedicated fitness center. For children, there are indoor and outdoor play areas, swimming pools, and sports classes. If you are looking to enjoy some sports with your loved ones, this is a great place where people of all ages can find something they enjoy.

CopenHill - CopenHill is a revolutionary sports and entertainment facility in Copenhagen and perhaps the only one of its kind in the world. It consists of an artificial skiing slope and a recreational hiking area built on top of a waste management center. The Amager Resource Center was established and 2017, and with it, CopenHill was launched. Here, you can bring your own ski or snowboard and enjoy the slopes or rent out equipment at CopenHill from the local shop *Steep and Deep.* After a good day of skiing or hiking, you can enjoy a meal at the CopenHills café and bar.

Address: Vindmøllevej 6, 2300 København, Denmark

CopenHot - CopenHot offers a unique spa experience. Here, the spas and saunas are outdoors under the open sky. Some are even hot tubs in a boat so you can enjoy sailing along the Copenhagen harbor as you soak in your spa. Moreover, they also offer ice baths, so if your wood-fired hot tub is getting too warm, you can cool off in a wooden-barrel ice bath. Even though the spa and sauna are under the open sky, the facility is open year-round. The wood-fired hot tubs ensure you don't feel cold even in the freezing winter months. A unique experience to enjoy.

Address: Refshalevej 204, 1432 København, Denmark

ACCOMMODATION

Hotels - Bronshoj and Vanlose offer a selection of high to mid-range hotels. These provide excellent amenities and convenient access to local attractions. They can be slightly more expensive than other options. However, they provide convenience and easy access to key areas.

TosleepinCPH Address: Gennemløbet 19, 2720 København, Denmark

Bed and Breakfasts – In Vanlose and Bronshoj, many boutique bed and breakfasts offer charming and personalized accommodation experiences. These are often in historic buildings or unique properties where you get personalized services and homemade meals. B&Bs provide a touch of local charm with a cozy and unique stay experience.

Royaltybed Copenhagen Address: Tornestykket 9, 2720 København, Denmark

9

ITINERARIES AND PROGRAMS

This chapter looks at potential itineraries and programs covering each district in Copenhagen. With these plans, you will experience the best of each district in a streamlined manner. Here are a few ideas on how to structure your visit to Copenhagen.

INDRE BY

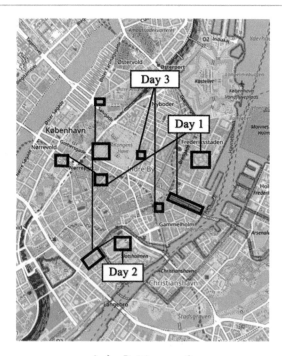

Indre By itinerary.[48]

DAY 1

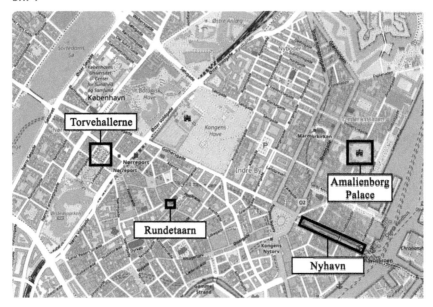

Day 1.[49]

Morning: Kick things off with a hearty breakfast at a café near your accommodations. Head over to Nyhavn and marvel at the colorful buildings and harbor.

Nyhavn QR Code.

Afternoon: Visit Amalienborg Palace and explore the Amalienborg Museum before heading to Torvehallerne for lunch.

Walk 600 m from Nyhavn to get to Amalienborg Palace. The Amalienborg Museum is 26 m away from Amalienborg Palace. To get to Torvehallerne, walk 300 m from the Amalienborg Museum to Marmorkirken metro stop and take M4 (Kobenhavn Syd St.) to the Kongens Nytorv stop. From there, take M1 (Vanlose St.) to Norreport and walk 130 m to Torvehallerne.

Amalienborg Palace and Museum QR Code.

Torvehallerne QR Code.

Evening: Head to Rundetaarn (the Round Tower) to enjoy panoramic views of the city.

Walk 600 m from Torvehallerne to get to Rundetaarn.

Rundetaarn QR Code.

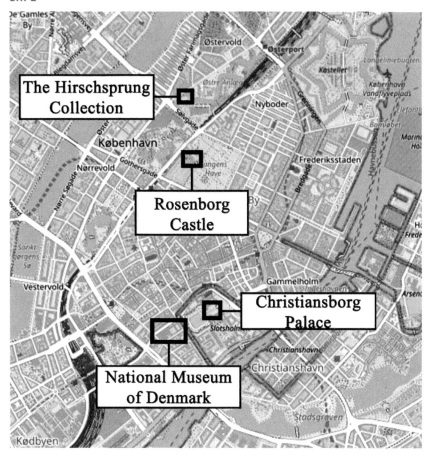

Day 2.[50]

Morning: Have breakfast near your accommodation then head to Rosenborg Castle. After, explore the Hirschsprung Collection to discover a large collection of Danish art from the 19th and early 20th centuries.

Walk 750 m from Rosenborg Castle via Solvgade Street to get to The Hirschsprung Collection.

Rosenborg Casle QR Code.

The Hirschsprung Collection QR Code.

Afternoon: Have lunch at Aamanns then head to the National Museum of Denmark.

National Museum of Denmark QR Code.

Evening: Explore Christiansborg Palace before taking a stroll along the canals of Copenhagen. Eat at one of the many eateries along the canal.

Walk 550 m from the National Museum of Denmark to get to Christiansborg Palace.

Christiansborg Palace QR Code.

DAY 3

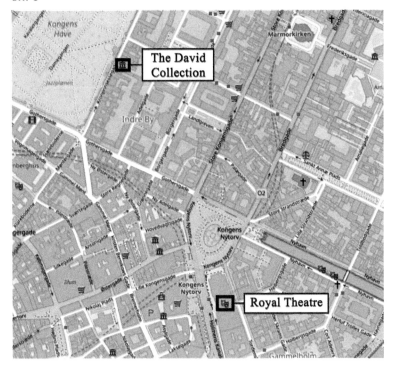

The David Collection

Royal Theatre

Day 3.[51]

Morning: Have breakfast at a café on the Oresund Strait to take in the beautiful sea views.

Afternoon: Return to Copenhagen and head over to the David Collection Museum. This museum features Islamic, European 18th century, and Danish modern art. This museum has one of Europe's most extensive collections of Islamic art and features exquisite artifacts not found anywhere else.

The David Collection Museum QR Code.

Evening: Unwind and catch a show at the Royal Theatre.

Walk 300 m to the Kronprinsessegade (Solvgade) bus stop and take bus 23 to Kongens Nytorv St. then walk 190 m to the Royal Theatre.

Royal Theater QR Code.

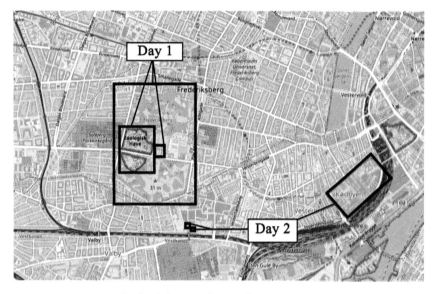

Frederiksberg and Vesterbro itinerary.[52]

DAY 1

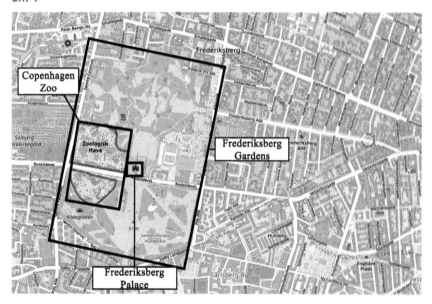

Day 1.[53]

Morning: Head to the Frederiksberg Gardens, a beautiful place to start your journey exploring the large open spaces and scenic views. Next door is the Frederiksberg Palace, a significant landmark in Copenhagen. Consider joining a guided tour covering this historic structure's history and architecture to learn more about the palace.

Walk 400 m from the Frederiksberg Gardens to the Frederiksberg Palace.

Frederiksberg Gardens QR Code.   **Frederiksberg Palace QR Code.**

Afternoon: Explore the Copenhagen Zoo and have lunch at a local restaurant nearby.

Walk 260 m from Frederiksberg Palace to the Copenhagen Zoo.

Copenhagen Zoo QR Code.

Evening: Visit the Frederiksberg Alle to browse shops and enjoy awe-inspiring architecture. The street is dotted with cafes and eateries where you can sample coffee with delicious Danish pastries. Bring the night to an end at the Frederiksberg Theatre and enjoy a variety of performances. Typically, plays, ballet, or concerts are performed at this venue.

Walk 50 m from the Copenhagen Zoo to the Zoolisk Have (Roskildevej) bus stop and take bus 7A (Sjaelor St.) to Frederiksberg Alle St.

DAY 2

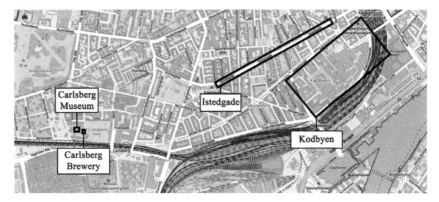

Day 2.[54]

Morning: Begin your day in the Meatpacking District, which has seen growth and development. Visit the Home of Carlsberg (formerly Carlsberg Brewery) to learn about the brewing process and sample fresh beer.

Walk 550 m to the Dybbolsbro metro stop and take Line C (Frederikssund St.) to Calsberg, then walk 400 m to the Carlsberg Brewery.

Meat Packing District QR Code.

Carlsberg Brewery QR Code.

Afternoon: Visit Enghave Park, where you can have a relaxing picnic and enjoy nature.

Walk 500 m to Sjaelor Boulevard (Vigerslev Alle) bus stop and take bus 1A (Hellerup St.) to Enghave Plads St. (Enghavevej), then walk 200 m to get to Engahevparken.

Enghave Park QR Code.

Evening: Stroll down Istedgade, Vesterbro's main street. You will find a mix of shops, cafes, and bars. Relax, unwind, have a snack, and capture Vesterbro's spirit in this diverse and lively atmosphere.

Walk 1 km from Enghave Park to get to Istedgade.

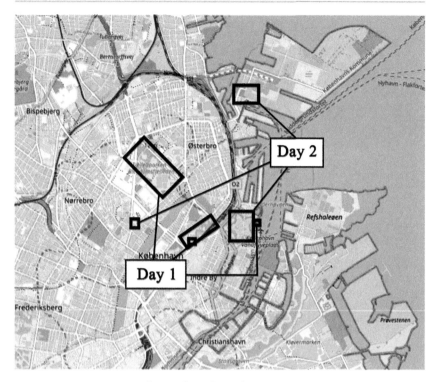

Osterbro and Nordre Frihavn itinerary.[55]

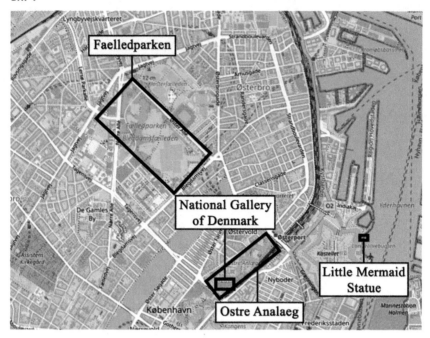

Day 1.[56]

Morning: Start the day with a jog or stroll in the Faelledparken in Osterbro. Spend quality time at the Lake Pavilion, soaking in the peace, quiet, and beautiful views. Next, explore the walking tracks around Osterbro's lakes, a popular spot with locals.

Faelledparken QR Code.

Lunch: Grab a bite to eat and head to the National Gallery of Denmark to explore the massive collection of Danish art and international art. Across the street from the gallery is the Ostre Anlaeg Park, which offers tranquil lakes where you can enjoy a peaceful lunch break, and there are several eateries in the area where you can enjoy a meal in the park.

Walk 500 m from Ostre Anlaeg to the National Gallery of Denmark.

National Gallery of Denmark   **Ostre Anlaeg QR Code.**

Evening: Go to the Langelinie, a beautiful waterfront area. Enjoy a leisurely walk and visit the famous Little Mermaid Statue.

Walk 600 m to the Osterport St. (Oslo Plads) bus stop and take bus 27 (Faergeterminal Sondre Frihavn) to Indiakaj, then walk 500 m to arrive at Langelinie.

Little Mermaid Statue QR Code.

DAY 2

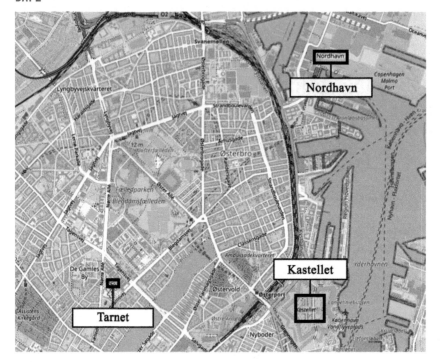

Day 2.[57]

Morning: Begin your day at Kastellet (The Citadel), a well-preserved military fortress and one of Copenhagen's iconic landmarks. Enjoy a meal at a nearby café.

Kastellet QR Code.

Afternoon: Head over to Nordhavn, a popular waterfront district. Stroll along the harbor and explore the modern buildings featuring dynamic and modern architecture. Have lunch at a nearby restaurant.

Nordhavn QR Code.

Evening: Visit the Tarnet (The Tower) at the Christiansborg Palace, which offers incredible views of Copenhagen. You can conveniently take an elevator to the top and enjoy a view of the entire city.

Tarnet QR Code.

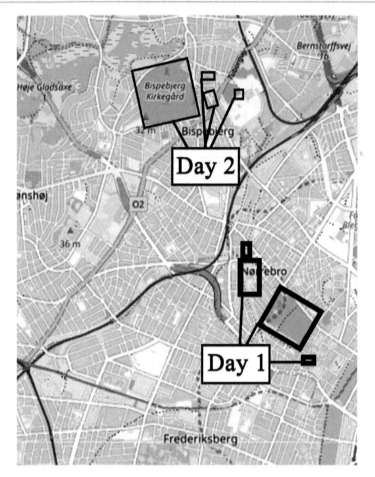

Nørrebro and Bispebjerg itinerary.[58]

DAY 1

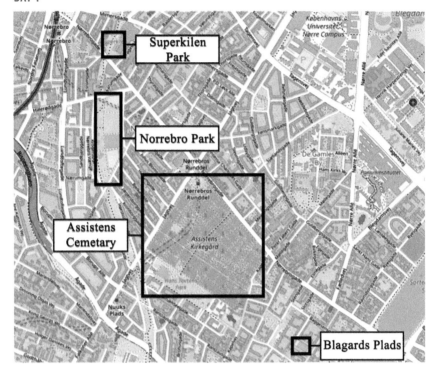

Day 1.[59]

Morning: Start your tour with a visit to the Assistens Cemetery. Next, head over to the Jaegersborggade. This is the main entertainment street in the district and is filled with boutique stores, artisan shops, and cafes where you can experience Norrebro's vibrant energy.

Walk 130 m from Assistens Cemetery to Jaeggersborggade.

Assistens Cemetery QR Code.

Afternoon: Buy a snack or lunch, and take it with you to enjoy at the Norrebro Parken. Alternatively, you can head to Superkilen Park, a uniquely designed park divided into color-coded zones.

Norrebro Park QR Code.

Superkilen Park QR Code.

Evening: Head to Blagards Plads, a bustling square in the Norrebro district known for cultural events and a lively atmosphere. Enjoy the live music, street performances, and many cafes and bars.

Blagards Plads QR Code.

DAY 2

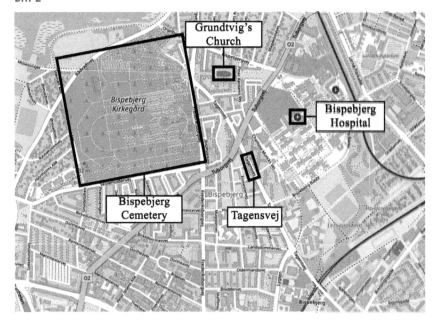

Day 2.[60]

Morning: Start your day with a visit to Grundtvig's Church, a classic historic building and a fine example of expressionist architecture. Next, visit the Bispebjerg Cemetery, best known for its cherry blossom avenue and natural beauty.

Walk 230 m to the Bispebjerg Torv (Tagensvej) bus stop and take bus 6A (Emdrup Torv) to Bispebjerg Parkalle then walk 900 m to the Bispebjerg Cemetery.

Grundtvig's Church QR Code.

Bispebjerg Cemetery QR Code.

Afternoon: Visit the Bispebjerg Hospital to admire its gardens. With little nooks for relaxing, an assortment of flower beds, and wildlife to be found, it has a very peaceful atmosphere.

Walk 900 m to the Bispebjerg Parkalle bus stop and take bus 6A (Norreport St.) to Bispebjerg Hospital (Tagensvej), then walk 500 m to the Bispebjerg Hospital.

Bispebjerg Hospital QR Code.

Evening: Bring the day to an end with a stroll along Tagensvej Street, a main street in Bispebjerg. This street has several eateries where you can enjoy dinner, coffee, or dessert.

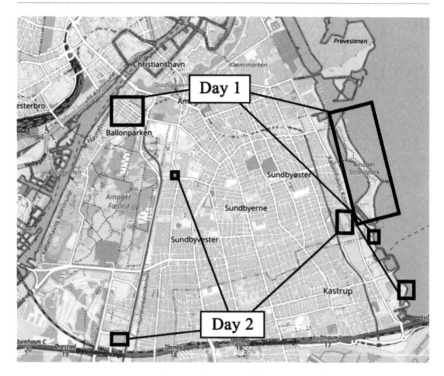

Amager East and Amager West itinerary.[61]

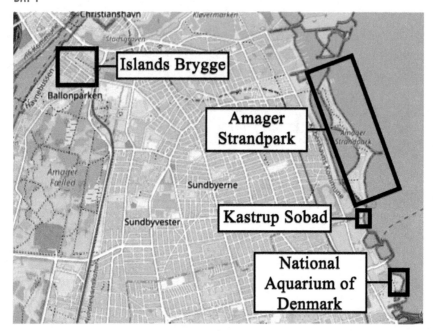

Day 1.[62]

Morning: Kick off your journey in Amager with a visit to Amager Strandpark, a large beach park with beaches, dunes, and grassy areas. Walk along the scenic coast, swim in the clear waters, or rent a boat or paddleboard for water-based fun. It's a beautiful natural oasis perfect for outdoor activities and relaxation.

Amager Strandpark QR Code.

Afternoon: Visit the Kastrup Sea Bath, known as *The Snail* due to its design. Then, head over to the National Aquarium of Denmark and explore a wide variety of marine life. The aquarium offers an immersive and educational experience, with interactive exhibits that are highly entertaining.

Walk 1.3 km from Amager Strandpark to Kastrup Sea Bath. To get to the National Aquarium of Denmark, walk 1.1 km from Kastrup Sea Bath.

Kastrup Sea Bath QR Code.

National Aquarium of Denmark QR Code.

Evening: Visit Islands Brygge, a vibrant part of town along the harbor. Enjoy a walk along the promenade or stop at a cafe or bar for a sundowner.

To get to Islands Brygge, walk 900 m from the National Aquarium of Denmark to Kastrup St. (Metro) and take line M2 (Vanlose St.) to Amager Strand. Walk about three minutes to Engvej (Italiensvej) bus stop and take bus 77 (Bella Center) to Kigkurren (Sturlasgade), then walk 270 m to Islands Brygge.

Islands Brygge QR Code.

DAY 2

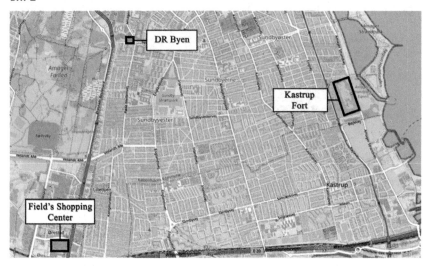

Day 2.[63]

Morning: Visit the DR Byen, the headquarters of the Danish National Broadcasting Corporation, to learn about Danish television and radio production and see the concert hall designed by Jean Nouvel.

DR Byen QR Code.

Afternoon: The Field's Shopping Center is one of Denmark's largest shopping malls and your next stop. This massive establishment has enough entertainment to keep you busy for several hours and a wonderful food court for snacks or a meal. You can find everything from home goods to fashion and electronics in this mall. It's a great shopping experience and also fun just to explore the shopping center.

Walk 240 m from DR Byen to the DR Byen metro stop and take line M1 Vestamager St. to Orestad then walk 110 m to Field's.

Field's Shopping Center QR Code.

Evening: Head over to the Kastrup Fort, a historic fortification turned into a recreational area. Explore the fort's grounds and enjoy the Oresund Strait views. There is a nearby park where you can unwind and relax.

Walk 140 m from Field's Shopping Center to Orestad bus stop and take bus 804 (Helsingborg C) to Kobenhavn Lufthavn and walk 1 min to Kobenhavms Lufthavn St. Metro and take line M2 (Vanlose St.) to Femoren St. Walk 650 m to the Kastrup Fortress.

Kastrup Fort QR Code.

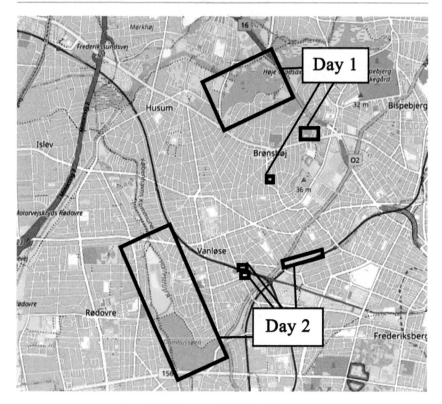

Bronshoj-Husum and Vanlose itinerary.[64]

DAY 1

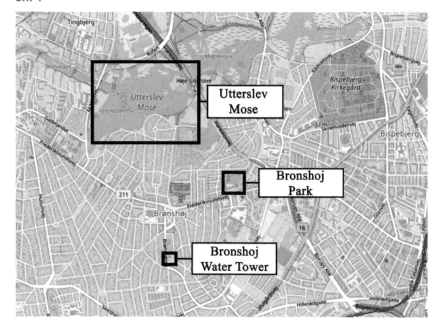

Day 1.[65]

Morning: Begin your journey with a visit to Utterslev Mose, a large nature reserve with lakes, wetlands, and abundant wildlife.

Utterslev Mose QR Code.

Afternoon: Head over to the iconic Bronshoj Water Tower, an architectural and historical landmark, to marvel at panoramic views of the city.

Walk 950 m from Utterslev Mose to Husumvold Kirke (Akandevej), take bus 2A (Refshaleoen) to Vallovej (Bronshojvej), and walk 190 m to the Bronshoj Water Tower.

Bronshoj Water Tower QR Code.

Evening: Casually walk through Bronshoj Park. This is a beautiful park featuring playgrounds and a pond. If you have children, they can have fun at the playground while you relax by the pond and recharge for the following day. It's a wonderful family-friendly outing, providing splendid natural beauty and recreational activities.

Walk 200 m from the Bronshoj Water Tower to the Vallovej (Bronshojvej) bus stop and take bus 2A (Tingbjerg Gavlhusvej) to Bronshoj Torv (Krappesholm-vej) and walk 750 to Bronshoj Park.

Bronshoj Park QR Code.

DAY 2

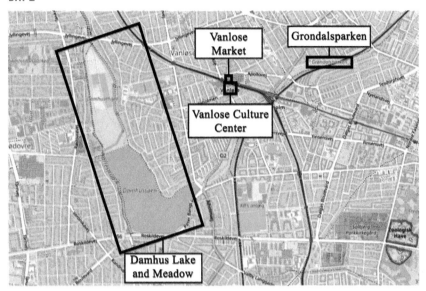

Day 2.[66]

Morning: Begin your day with a visit to Damhus Lake and the Damhus Meadow. which are great spaces for outdoor activities. You can relax by the lake or enjoy a wide-open meadow for sports and activities.

Damhus Lake and Meadow QR Code.

Afternoon: Visit the Vanlose Culture Center, attend workshops, participate in ongoing events, and watch performances. Then, if you happen to be visiting on a Saturday, head to the Vanlose Flea Market to find a unique souvenir.

Walk 750 m from Damhus Meadow to Hyltebjerg Alle (Alekistevej) and take bus 10 (Bronshoj Torv) to Vanlose St., Jydeholmen, and walk 130 m to Vanlose Culture Center. Walk 240 m from Vanlose Culture Center to Vanlose Market.

Vanlose Culture Center QR Code.

Vanlose Market QR Code.

Evening: Head to Grondal's Park, which has playgrounds, sports facilities, and green areas where you can relax. You can enjoy a leisurely walk through the park or unwind in the green spaces while the kids play in the playground.

Walk 21 m from Vanlose Market to Vaslose St.bus stop and take bus 9A (Kongens Enghave Valbyparken) to A.D. Jorgensens vej. Then, walk 400 m to Grondal's Park.

Grondal's Park QR Code.

10

DAY TRIPS BEYOND THE CITY

Copenhagen City offers much to see and do. However, there are more attractions nearby that are also worth a visit. This chapter covers the best of Copenhagen's vicinities that are easy to reach in an hour or two. Insider tips and tricks to make your trip more convenient and enjoyable are provided.

LOUISIANA MUSEUM OF MODERN ART

The Louisiana Museum of Modern Art is in Humlebaek. The museum is renowned for its extensive modern and contemporary art collection. Moreover, the museum's situation has beautiful green and natural surroundings with incredible views of the Oresund Strait. There is a splendid sculpture park and an interactive children's play area nearby.

The Louisiana Museum of Modern Art.[67]

TRANSPORT OPTIONS

Train – This is the quickest way to the museum. Take the regional train to Helsingor from the Copenhagen Central Station. Get off at the Humlebaek station, which is roughly a 40-minute journey. As you exit the station, head east on the Humlebark Strandvej and follow the road signs to the museum. It is a pleasant 10-minute walk from the station.

Car – It will take around 40-60 minutes by car, depending on traffic conditions. Get on the E47 highway and drive north from Copenhagen. You can find free car parking at the museum. There is additional parking space around the museum at peak times.

Cycle – You can cycle from Copenhagen to the museum. There is a well-marked, scenic 22-mile cycling track along the coast. A one-way journey typically takes two hours.

ACTIVITIES

You can enjoy various activities at the museum. The top options include:

Art Collection – Revered artists' works, including Giacometti, Warhol, and Picasso, are displayed in the museum. The permanent collection holds more than 3500 pieces. The museum frequently hosts ex-

hibitions that showcase additional artworks. You can find information about upcoming exhibitions on the museum's website.

Sculpture Park – Art meets nature in the sculpture park. This is a delightful outdoor space on the museum's grounds with pieces by artists such as Henry Moore and Alexander Calder. Guided tours are offered to learn more about the individual sculptures and the artists.

Children's Wing – If you are traveling with children, they will enjoy this area the most. It has several creative activities and interactive stations explicitly for children. There are workshops introducing kids to the many art forms.

Cafe and Museum Shop – You can enjoy a meal or a snack at the café and take in the spectacular sea views. Nearby is the museum shop to buy souvenirs, art books, and design gifts.

TIPS

✦ *The best time to visit is on weekdays in the early hours. Weekends and holidays are typically busy.*

✦ *Visit in the spring or summer to enjoy the outdoor sculpture park. It is open in winter, but summer is the best weather.*

+ The museum is usually open Tuesday to Friday from 11 am to 10 pm and on weekends from 11 am to 6 pm. It is closed on Mondays, but hours may vary, so check before visiting.

+ Purchase tickets online to skip the line. Students, seniors, and groups can get discounts. The museum offers free admission for certain age groups. Check the website before visiting to see available offers.

Address: Gl Strandvej 13, 3050 Humlebæk, Denmark

ROSKILDE

Roskilde is one of the most iconic cities in Denmark, known for its history and culture. It's not too far from Copenhagen and a must-visit for anyone interested in history, culture, and Vikings. The city is best known for the iconic Viking Ship Museum and the UNESCO-listed Roskilde Cathedral. Moreover, if you visit in the summer, go to the Roskilde Festival, one of Europe's biggest music festivals.

Roskilde Cathedral.[68]

TRANSPORT OPTIONS

Train – The train will be the quickest and most convenient way to get to Roskilde from Copenhagen. Take the InterCity regional train from Copenhagen Central Station to Roskilde. It is about a 25-minute ride, and trains depart from the central station regularly throughout the day. When you leave Roskilde station head southwest toward Kongevej to the city center. Nearly all the main attractions are within walking distance.

Car – Alternatively, you can travel by car using Route 21 from Copenhagen. This journey will take approximately 40 minutes, depending on traffic. You will find ample parking near the Viking Ship Museum and other parking spaces throughout the city center.

Bicycle – A bike ride from Copenhagen to Roskilde takes about 2 hours. This scenic ride goes through the countryside and weaves through small towns on the border.

ACTIVITIES

Viking Ship Museum – The Viking Ship Museum is one of the most exciting establishments in Roskilde to explore. You'll find original Viking ships that were excavated from the Roskilde Fjord. There are exhibits, reconstructions, and interactive displays illustrating Viking culture and the ships' history and significance. From May to September, there are boat trips in reconstructed Viking-style boats, which are an experience to remember.

Roskilde Cathedral – A short walk from the museum is the Roskilde Cathedral, a stunning example of Gothic architecture and a UNESCO World Heritage site. It is the burial site of several Danish monarchs and royal family members. The cathedral's architecture reflects over 800 years of Danish history. Tombs, chapels, and a beautifully designed altar are housed inside the cathedral. You can visit the cathedral towers and see the breathtaking panoramic views of Roskilde.

Roskilde Festival – If you are visiting in late June or early July then the Roskilde Festival is something you certainly will want to visit. It's one of Europe's largest music festivals and attracts visitors from around the world. Even if you are not a big music fan, it is worth attending to experience the atmosphere. Tickets sell out quickly, so booking in advance is essential.

Lejre Museum – The Lejre Museum is outside Roskilde and offers a deep dive into Danish history and mythology. Around the museum are several archeological sites, including burial grounds and stone circles. The museum is dedicated to the Kings of Lehre, who ruled Denmark before the Vikings. The museum is surrounded by beautiful landscapes with walking trails.

Roskilde Harbor – Be sure to visit Roskilde Harbor, where you can enjoy tranquil views of the Roskilde Fjord. The harbor has plenty of cafes and restaurants where you can relax, refuel, and enjoy the views. There are water activities, like boat rentals, to explore the fjord on your own.

TIPS

✦ *Roskilde is a great place to visit year-round, but spring and summer are particularly suitable for outdoor activities. If you are interested in the festival, plan your trip around June and July.*

✦ *If you are visiting in the summer, purchase tickets for the Viking Ship Museum and Roskilde Cathedral in advance. You can usually find combination tickets and ticket deals online to save you a lot of money.*

✦ *There are many beautiful views to capture and several exhibits, such as the Viking ships, the cathedral's interior, and the harbor.*

Elsinore (locally known as Helsingor) is a beautiful coastal city just outside Copenhagen. This city is most famous for the Kronborg Castle, which was the setting for Shakespeare's famous play *Hamlet*. In addition to the castle, the city offers fascinating views across the Oresund Strait and museums. Located on the coast, Elsinore is quite close to the neighboring country, Sweden.

Kronborg Castle.[69]

TRANSPORT OPTIONS

Train - The easiest and most scenic way to get to Elsinore is by train. You can take the regional train from Copenhagen Central Station to Helsingor station. This is a 55-minute journey covering beautiful views of the Oresund Strait. Once you arrive at Helsingor, the city center and main attractions are within walking distance. Kronborg Castle is roughly a 10-minute walk from the station.

Car - When traveling by car, head north on the E47 highway from Copenhagen to Helsingor. The drive usually takes an hour, depending on traffic conditions. Once in Helsingor, you can easily find parking near the Kronborg Castle and in other areas in the city center.

Ferry – If you want to enjoy the maritime experience to the fullest, then take a ferry ride from Helsingor across the Öresund Strait to Helsingborg in Sweden. The ferry ride is roughly 20 minutes one-way and offers the best views of the Danish coastline.

ACTIVITIES

Kronborg Castle – Begin your trip to Elsinore with a visit to the Kronborg Castle, a UNESCO world heritage site. The castle's structure and surrounding moat offer a glimpse into the military history and royal culture. Explore the grand halls, royal apartments, and the famous ballroom at the castle. Consider exploring the casemates beneath the castle where soldiers once lived and worked in the damp, dark underground chambers. Within the castle, there are intricate tapestries depicting the Danish kings and several exhibits throughout the castle telling tales of the history and grandeur of the establishment. Learn about the castle's strategic significance and how it played a major role in shaping the history of the country.

Maritime Museum of Denmark – This museum is a short walk from the Kronborg Castle and is Denmark's biggest and best museum regarding maritime history. The museum's structure is an architectural marvel built in an underground dry dock. It features interactive exhibits and models of historic ships. It houses several displays telling the story of Denmark's maritime heritage, from Viking ships to modern shipping.

Culture Yard – Adjacent to the Maritime Museum, the Culture Yard is a vibrant space dedicated to Danish art, theater, and music. The establishment is housed in a former shipyard building and is a popular venue for local events. Check the schedule, as there are always live performances, concerts, workshops, and exhibitions happening.

Helsingor City Center – The Helsingor city center is a relic from the past, characterized by cobblestone streets, charming old-style squares, and timber houses. The pedestrian-friendly streets are lined with boutique shops, local markets, and cafes. In the city center is St. Olaf's Church, a well-preserved 13th-century church known for its Gothic architecture and highly detailed altarpiece. For a truly local experience, visit Axeltorv Square in the city center, which is the venue for a market where you can find local produce and traditional Danish goods.

✦ *The best time to visit Helsingor is in the summer when outdoor activities and festivities are in full swing. The live Hamlet* performance at the Kronborg Castle is from June to August. The winter is enjoyable as the city takes on a cozy atmosphere, but it's not quite as busy as in the summer, with fewer things to do.

✦ If you want family fun, then Helsingor is a great choice, as there are plenty of places where you'll find dedicated amenities and facilities for children.

✦ Visit the Kronborg Castle gardens, as they offer a fantastic green open space where you can have a picnic or enjoy outdoor activities.

THE CLIFFS OF MON

The Cliffs of Mon (locally known as Mons Klint) are a stunning natural wonder in Denmark. These towering white cliffs stand right next to the Baltic Sea's bright blue waters, creating a stunning view. Moreover, this location is rich in geological history and offers several opportunities for entertaining outdoor activities. Anyone looking to get into nature or for an outdoor adventure should visit the Cliffs of Mon.

Mons Klint.[70]

TRANSPORT OPTIONS

Car – The quickest way to get to the Cliffs of Mon from Copenhagen is by car. From Copenhagen, get onto the E47 highway and head south toward the island of Mon. Once you arrive at Mons, follow the directions to Mons Klint. The final leg of the journey will take you through the Danish countryside through rolling hills and small towns. The journey takes about 2 hours, depending on traffic.

Train and Bus – If you want to use public transport, take a train from Copenhagen Central to Vordingborg Station. This leg of the journey takes about an hour. From Vordingborg, catch bus 660R, heading to Stege. From Stege, transfer to bus 667, which will take you directly to Mons Klint. The travel time for public transport is roughly 3 hours, depending on how quickly you can find transport.

Cycling – Cycling is a great option, but only possible from Stege (the main town in Mon) to Mons Klint. You will need to get to Stege by car, bus, or train, and then you can cycle to Mons Klint, which is only 12 miles away. This is about an hour's ride from Stege, with some great views on the way.

ACTIVITIES

Mons Klint Hiking Trails – There are several hiking trails in the Mont Klint area, with varying difficulty levels. The great thing about these trails is they weave through the cliffs and the surrounding forests, giving you a taste of both environments. Many trails go to the edge of the cliff, giving you an incredible view of the sea below. Some trails are quite challenging, so be prepared for steep inclines and stairs. The forest trails are less demanding and particularly good for the summer as there is plenty of shade.

GeoCenter Mons Klint – Located near the top of the cliffs, the Geo-Center is an interactive museum dedicated to Mons Klint's geological history. Here, you can learn about the area's natural significance. You will learn how these cliffs came to be, and the fossils found in the area.

Kayaking and Boating – Kayaking and boating tours are available at Mons Klint, where you can explore the cliffs from a different viewpoint. The waters near the cliffs are quite calm, so it's a great place for beginners to try kayaking.

Liselund Manor Park - Liselund Park is close to the Mons Klint and has an 18th-century manor house on its grounds. It's a great place to relax and unwind and soak in the natural atmosphere. Stroll through the gardens, enjoy the area, and visit the small manor house to explore the 18th-century architecture. However, the building is closed to visitors.

Liselund Manor Park.[71]

Beaches of Mon – The island of Mon has several sandy beaches. However, these are best visited in the summer months. In winter the weather and water temperature make it less than ideal. In summer, you can enjoy swimming, sunbathing, and picnicking. One of the best beaches to visit is Rabylille or Ulvshale Beach.

TIPS

+ *The best time to visit is late spring to early autumn (May to September) when the weather is mild and the trails are dry. Weekdays and early mornings are the best time to visit if you don't want to run into a crowd.*

+ *While this is a family-friendly area, keeping an eye on kids and the elderly near the cliff areas and the water is essential.*

+ *If you plan on hiking, bring a pair of sturdy hiking shoes, as the trails and the terrain can be rough.*

+ *In the summer, bring a hat, sunscreen, and plenty of water.*

BONUS CHAPTER: USEFUL DANISH SURVIVAL PHRASES

Language is a primary concern when visiting countries where English is not the native language. Luckily, Danes are familiar with English and enjoy communicating with anyone facing trouble with Danish. Nearly 90% of Danes understand and can speak English. If you are in a big urban area like Copenhagen, you won't have a communication problem. However, knowing local phrases is always advantageous.

This chapter includes the common phrases and is divided into categories. This way, you can refer to them quickly, depending on your needs.

Danish has its own alphabet and pronunciation. In this list of survival phrases, note the phonetic pronunciation of each phrase to ensure you get your message across correctly.

EVERYDAY PHRASES

In this section are basic everyday phrases for casual conversation.

+ **Hello:** *Hej (Hi)*
+ **Goodbye:** *Farvel (Far-vel)*
+ **Good morning:** *Godmorgen (Go-morn)*
+ **Good evening:** *Godaften (Go-daften)*
+ **Please:** *Venligst / Vær venlig (Ven-list / Vare ven-lee)*
+ **Thank you:** *Tak (Tak)*
+ **You're welcome:** *Selv tak (Selv tak)*
+ **Excuse me:** *Undskyld mig (Oon-skool mai)*
+ **Yes:** *Ja (Ya)*
+ **No:** *Nej (Nai)*

+ **Do you speak English?:** *Taler du engelsk? (Tay-ler do eng-elsk)*

+ **I don't understand:** *Jeg forstår ikke (Yai for-stor ikke)*

+ **I'm sorry:** *Jeg er ked af det (Yai er keel ah de)*

DINING

Here are common phrases that may come in handy at a restaurant or cafe.

+ **I would like...:** *Jeg vil gerne have... (Yai vil GEAR-nuh have...)*

+ **How much does this cost?:** *Hvor meget koster det? (Vor MY-it KOS-tuh deh?)*

+ **Can I get the check, please?:** *Må jeg få regningen, tak? (Moh yai foh rai-ning-en, tak?)*

+ **Where is the bathroom?:** *Hvor er toilettet? (Vor air toy-LET-et?)*

+ **Is this seat taken?:** *Er denne plads optaget? (Air DEN-neh plahs op-TAH-get?)*

+ **A table for two, please:** *Et bord til to, tak (Et bor til toh, tak)*

+ **Can I see the menu?:** *Må jeg se menukortet? (Moh yai say men-yu-kor-det)*

+ **What do you recommend?:** *Hvad anbefaler du? (Vel an-befay-ler do)*

+ **I am a vegetarian:** *Jeg er vegetar (Yai er vege-tar)*

+ **Water, please:** *Vand, tak (Van, tak)*

+ **The bill, please:** *Regningen, tak (Rai-ning-en, tak)*

+ **Delicious:** *Lækkert (Lek-kert)*

+ **Can I have the check, please?:** *Kan jeg få regningen, tak? (Kan yai fo rai-ning-en, tak)*

SHOPPING

Here are phrases useful for shopping.

+ **How much does this cost?:** *Hvor meget koster dette? (Vor MY-it KOS-tuh DEH-tuh?)*

+ **I would like to buy this:** *Jeg vil gerne købe dette (Yai vil GEAR-nuh KØ-buh DEH-tuh)*

- ✦ **Do you accept credit cards?**: *Tager I imod kreditkort? (TAH-yer ee ee-MOOL kredit-KORT?)*
- ✦ **Where can I find...?**: *Hvor kan jeg finde...? (Vor kan yai FIN-neh...?)*
- ✦ **Can I try this on?**: *Må jeg prøve dette? (Moh yai PROW-uh DEH-tuh?)*
- ✦ **Is there a discount?**: *Er der rabat? (Air der rah-BAT?)*

TRANSPORTATION

Here are transportation-related phrases.

- ✦ **Where is the bus/train station?**: *Hvor er bus-/togstationen? (vor air bus/toh-STAY-shun-en?)*
- ✦ **How much is a ticket to...?**: *Hvor meget koster en billet til...? (vor MY-it KOS-tuh en bil-LET til...?)*
- ✦ **I need a taxi**: *Jeg har brug for en taxa (yay har broo for en TAX-ah)*
- ✦ **Can you help me?**: *Kan du hjælpe mig? (kan doo YEL-puh my?)*
- ✦ **I'm lost**: *Jeg er faret vild (yay air FAR-et vil)*
- ✦ **Where is...?**: *Hvor er...? (vor air...?)*
- ✦ **Which way to...?**: *Hvilken vej til...? (VIL-ken vie til...?)*
- ✦ **I would like to go to...**: *Jeg vil gerne til... (yay vil GEAR-nuh til...)*

ADDITIONAL PHRASES

Here are general phrases for everyday situations.

- ✦ **What time is it?**: *Hvad er klokken? (va er KLOK-en?)*
- ✦ **Nice to meet you**: *Rart at møde dig (rah-t at MØ-thuh die)*
- ✦ **Cheers!**: *Skål! (skohl!)*
- ✦ **Where are you from?**: *Hvor kommer du fra? (vor KOM-mer doo frah?)*
- ✦ **Can you take a photo of me/us**: *Kan du tage et billede af mig/os? (kan doo TAY-uh et BILL-uh-thuh af my/os?)*
- ✦ **Is this seat taken?**: *Er denne plads optaget? (air DEN-neh plahs op-TAH-get?)*

ACCOMMODATION

Here are phrases related to accommodation.

+ **I have a reservation**: *Jeg har en reservation (yay har en re-ser-VAH-syon)*

+ **Do you have a room available?**: *Har I et ledigt værelse? (har ee et LAY-deet VAY-ruh-suh)*

+ **What time is check-out?**: *Hvornår er check-out? (vor-NOHR air check-out?)*

+ **Can I get a wake-up call?**: *Kan jeg få et vækkeopkald? (kan yay foh et VAY-kuhp-kahl?)*

+ **Where is the elevator?**: *Hvor er elevatoren? (vor air eh-lee-VAH-tohr-en?)*

+ **Can I get some extra towels?**: *Kan jeg få nogle ekstra håndklæder? (kan yay foh NOH-gleh EK-stra HONK-ley-ther?)*

PHRASES FOR EMERGENCY SITUATIONS

Here are phrases for emergency situations.

+ **Call the police**: *Ring til politiet (ring til po-LEE-see-et)*

+ **I need a doctor**: *Jeg har brug for en læge (yay har broo for en LAY-uh)*

+ **Where is the nearest hospital?**: *Hvor er det nærmeste hospital? (vor air det NAIR-muh-stuh hos-pee-TAL?)*

+ **I'm allergic to...**: *Jeg er allergisk over for... (yay air al-LEHR-gisk OH-ver for...)*

+ **Help!**: *Hjælp! (yelp!)*

+ **Is there a pharmacy nearby?**: *Er der et apotek i nærheden? (air der et ah-po-TEK ee NAIR-hee-den?)*

+ **I'm lost**: *Jeg er faret vild (yay air FAH-ret vil)*

+ **Can you help me?**: *Kan du hjælpe mig? (kan doo YEL-pe my)*

APPENDIX

Aamanns 1921 – Mentioned in Chapters 3 and 9.

Amager Beachpark– Mentioned in Chapters 1, 7, and 9.

Amager Bio– Mentioned in Chapter 7.

Amager Centret– Mentioned in Chapter 7.

Amager Faelled – Mentioned in Chapters 1 and 7.

Amagerbrogade – Mentioned in Chapter 7.

Amalienborg Museum – Mentioned in Chapter 9.

Amalienborg Palace – Mentioned in Chapter 9.

Assistens Cemetery – Mentioned in Chapters 6 and 9.

Assistens Kirkegard Flea Market – Mentioned in Chapter 6.

Aveny T – Mentioned in Chapter 4.

Beaches on Mon – Mentioned in Chapter 10.

Bellahoj 72 Activity Center – Mentioned in Chapter 8.

Bellahoj Aqua Center – Mentioned in Chapter 8.

Bispebjerg Cemetery – Mentioned in Chapters 6 and 9.

Bispebjerg's Hospital's Botanical Garden – Mentioned in Chapter 6.

Blagards Plads – Mentioned in Chapters 6 and 9.

Borsen Stock Exchange – Mentioned in Chapters 1 and 3.

Bronshoj Torv – Mentioned in Chapter 8.

Bronshoj Water Tower – Mentioned in Chapters 6 and 9.

Brygge Harbor Bath – Mentioned in Chapter 1.

Café Bopa – Mentioned in Chapter 5.

Café Dyrehaven – Mentioned in Chapter 4.

Café Langebro – Mentioned in Chapter 8.

Carlsberg Brewery – Mentioned in Chapters 4, 9.

Grod – Mentioned in Chapter 6.

Grondal Multicenter – Mentioned in Chapter 8.

Grondalsparken – Mentioned in Chapters 8 and 9.

Grundtvig's Church – Mentioned in Chapters 6 and 9.

H3 Amager Fiskehus – Mentioned in Chapter 7.

Helsingor – Mentioned in Chapter 10.

Helsingor City Center – Mentioned in Chapter 10.

Il Buco – Mentioned in Chapter 7.

Illum – Mentioned in Chapter 3.

Islands Brygge – Mentioned in Chapter 7.

Islands Brygge Harbor Bath – Mentioned in Chapter 7.

Istedgade – Mentioned in Chapters 4 and 9.

Jaeggersborggade – Mentioned in Chapters 6, 9.

Kalvebod Faelled – Mentioned in Chapters 7, 8.

Kastellet – Mentioned in Chapters 1, 5, 9.

Kastrup Airport – Mentioned in Chapters 1 and 2.

Kastrup Fort – Mentioned in Chapter 9.

Kastrup Sobad – Mentioned in Chapters 7 and 9.

Kiin Kiin To Go – Mentioned in Chapter 5.

Klatreskoven – Mentioned in Chapter 8.

Kodbyen (Meatpacking District) – Mentioned in Chapters 4 and 9.

Kronborg Castle – Mentioned in Chapter 10.

La Neta – Mentioned in Chapter 6.

Lejre Museum – Mentioned in Chapter 10.

Liselund Manor Park – Mentioned in Chapter 10.

Louisiana Museum of Modern Art – Mentioned in Chapter 10.

Madhjornet – Mentioned in Chapter 8.

Magasin du Nord – Mentioned in Chapter 3.

Maritime Museum of Denmark – Mentioned in Chapter 10.

Meyers Bageri – Mentioned in Chapter 6.

Mielcke and Hurtigkarl – Mentioned in Chapter 4.

Mikkeller Bar – Mentioned in Chapter 4.

Mons Klint Hiking Trails – Mentioned in Chapter 10.

Mosen – Mentioned in Chapter 8.

National Museum of Denmark – Mentioned in Chapters 3 and 9.

Naturcenter Amager – Mentioned in Chapter 7.

Noma – Mentioned in Chapters 1, 3.

Nordic Nesting – Mentioned in Chapter 7.

Nordre Frihavnsgade – Mentioned in Chapter 5.

Norrebro Park – Mentioned in Chapters 8 and 9.

Norrebrogade – Mentioned in Chapter 6.

Norrebroparken – Mentioned in Chapter 6.

Nyhavn – Mentioned in Chapters 1, 3, and 9.

Oksnehallen – Mentioned in Chapter 4.

Orestad – Mentioned in Chapters 7 and 8.

Orstedsparken – Mentioned in Chapter 1.

Osterbro Stadium – Mentioned in Chapter 5.

Osterbrogade – Mentioned in Chapter 5.

Ostre Anlaeg Park – Mentioned in Chapters 5 and 9.

Packyard – Mentioned in Chapter 6.

Prags Boulevard – Mentioned in Chapter 7.

Refshaleoen – Mentioned in Chapters 7 and 9.

Restaurant Kadeau – Mentioned in Chapter 7.

Restaurant Karla – Mentioned in Chapter 3.

Restaurant Kreta III – Mentioned in Chapter 8.

Rosenberg Castle Gardens – Mentioned in Chapter 3.

Rosenborg Castle – Mentioned in Chapters 1, 3, and 9.

Roskilde – Mentioned in Chapter 10.

Roskilde Cathedral – Mentioned in Chapter 10.

Roskilde Festival – Mentioned in Chapter 10.

Roskilde Harbor – Mentioned in Chapter 10.

Royal Danish Theatre – Mentioned in Chapters 3 and 9.

Royal Golf Center – Mentioned in Chapter 7.

Rundetaarn Tower – Mentioned in Chapters 1, 3, and 9

Sonder Boulevard – Mentioned in Chapter 4.

Spindereit Shopping Center – Mentioned in Chapter 8.

Stroget – Mentioned in Chapter 3.

Superkilen Market – Mentioned in Chapter 6.

Superkilen Park – Mentioned in Chapters 6 and 9.

Svanemolle Beach – Mentioned in Chapter 5.

Tagensvej – Mentioned in Chapters 6 and 9.

Tarnet – Mentioned in Chapter 9.

Taverna Kreta – Mentioned in Chapter 8.

Telia Parken – Mentioned in Chapter 5.

The Black Market – Mentioned in Chapter 6.

The Blue Planet (National Aquarium of Denmark) – Mentioned in Chapters 7 and 9.

The Cliffs of Mon – Mentioned in Chapter 10.

The David Collection – Mentioned in Chapter 9.

The Design Museum Denmark – Mentioned in Chapter 5.

The Hirschsprung Collection – Mentioned in Chapters 3 and 9.

The Lakes – Mentioned in Chapter 5.

The Little Mermaid Statue – Mentioned in Chapters 5 and 9.

The Red Square – Mentioned in Chapter 6.

CONCLUSION

In this book, we have gone through Copenhagen extensively. Looking at the various districts that come together to make up the fantastic city of Copenhagen and also closely examining the unique features that each area has to offer.

Some key attractions include the Nyhavn Harbor, the Little Mermaid statue, the majestic Rosenborg Castle, and, of course, the beautiful Tivoli Gardens. Amorelso, the historic neighborhoods of Vesterbro, Indre By, and Norrebro, along with many others, we also looked at in detail in the guide.

Copenhagen is a place with a rich and detailed history where you can experience so many unique things. The diversity of experiences that this city offers is easily one of the major highlights. Whether you are into history, technology, or architecture or are one with an artistic flair, Copenhagen has something for everyone. The Amalienborg Palace, the Superkilen Park, the Copenhagen Opera House, and so much more! A place where old and new come together in a way that each maintains its individuality but also fits seamlessly with the other.

In Copenhagen, you will notice that tourists are in town all year round. However, to get the best experience, and especially to experience the outdoor activities, it is recommended you visit between May and September. During this time, the weather is mild, and outdoor activities are in full swing. If you do have to visit in the winter, then try adjusting your trip during or near Christmas time. At Christmastime, Copenhagen comes alive with festive markets such as those in Tivoli Gardens, along with many other festivities that are only found during Christmas time.

In Copenhagen, getting around is not a problem at all. There is a robust local transport system whether you need to travel within Copenhagen or you need to get from Copenhagen to another part of the country. The Metro is operational 24 hours a day, seven days a week, and has an excellent network that covers all parts of the city. Additionally, consider getting the Copenhagen Card which gives you unlimited access to public transport and also gets you free entry to many attractions.

When visiting Copenhagen be sure to make some time for the attractions located a little outside Copenhagen itself. As we discussed, areas such as Reffen, Assistens Cemetery, and Cisternerne in Frederiksberg are places that offer a once-in-a-lifetime experience. These are not too far from Copenhagen, and you can easily get there on public transport. In this guide, we have outlined an itinerary for getting to these out-of-cities locations; however, you can always customize the plan further to meet your needs.

Moreover, there are a number of festivals in Copenhagen that only happen once a year, such as the Copenhagen Jazz Festival. These are things you can plan for a future visit to Copenhagen if you won't be traveling during the event season. Alternatively, if you are traveling in the summer, you may want to plan a trip for the winter when you get to enjoy the winter atmosphere and the popular *hygge* atmosphere of Copenhagen.

Copenhagen is a city that leaves a lasting impression. Look into this guide to get some idea about how to plan your trip and make a visit to Copenhagen a reality.

Here's another book by Captivating Travels that you might like

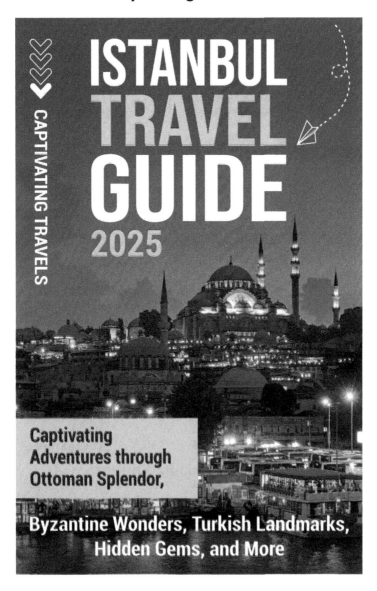

ISTANBUL TRAVEL GUIDE 2025

CAPTIVATING TRAVELS

Captivating Adventures through Ottoman Splendor, Byzantine Wonders, Turkish Landmarks, Hidden Gems, and More

Welcome Aboard, Discover
Your Limited-Time Free Bonus!

Hello, traveler! Welcome to the Captivating Travels family, and thanks for grabbing a copy of this book! Since you've chosen to join us on this journey, we'd like to offer you something special.

Check out the link below for a FREE Ultimate Travel Checklist eBook & Printable PDF to make your travel planning stress-free and enjoyable.

But that's not all - you'll also gain access to our exclusive email list with even more free e-books and insider travel tips. Well, what are you waiting for? Click the link below to join and embark on your next adventure with ease.

Access your bonus here: https://livetolearn.lpages.co/ checklist/

Or, Scan the QR code!

REFERENCES

10 Top Attractions in Bronshoj (2024). (n.d.). TRIP.COM. https://ph.trip.com/travel-guide/attraction/bronshoj-10369/tourist-attractions/type-forests-71-38375?locale=en_ph

A guide to shopping in Copenhagen. (n.d.). VisitDenmark. https://www.visit-denmark.com/denmark/things-do/shopping/copenhagen

Ago, R. #travel • 6 Y. (2018, March 2). Amager Fælled – Green Nature Oasis in the Danish Capital Copenhagen. Steemit. https://steemit.com/travel/@raci/amager-flled---green-nature-oasis-in-the-danish-capital-copenhagen-1519328995-2151597

amsted. (2019, May 24). what to do in Amager. Amager Village. https://amagervillage.org/tag/what-to-do-in-amager/

Area guide: Family-friendly Østerbro. (n.d.). VisitCopenhagen. https://www.visitcopenhagen.com/oesterbro

Area guide: Nørrebro. (n.d.). VisitCopenhagen. https://www.visitcopenhagen.com/noerrebro

ATTRACTIONS. (2022). Copenhagencard.com. https://copenhagencard.com/attractions/651

Barsoe , A. M. (2021, June 10). Time Out Magazine: Copenhagen's Nørrebro district is the coolest in the world. Wonderful Copenhagen. https://www.wonderfulcopenhagen.com/wonderful-copenhagen/international-press/time-out-magazine-copenhagens-norrebro-district-coolest-world

Best Things to Do in Amager | Unique Tours & Activities – Denmark. (n.d.). Airbnb. https://www.airbnb.com/amager-denmark/things-to-do

Beth. (2023, November 20). First Timers Guide To The Best Food In Copenhagen – Traverse. Https://Www.traverse-Blog.com. https://www.traverse-blog.com/best-restaurants-copenhagen/

Bronshoj-Husum, Denmark – Facts and information on Bronshoj-Husum – Denmark.Places-in-the-world.com. (n.d.). Denmark.places-In-The-World.com. https://denmark.places-in-the-world.com/6949460-place-bronshoj-husum.html

Charlottehaven | Your guide to Østerbro. (n.d.). Www.charlottehaven.com. https://www.charlottehaven.com/dk/en/hotel/articles/out-about/your-guide-to-oesterbro/

Climer , B. (2023, May 21). My Guide to Copenhagen's Public Transportation – Fund for Education Abroad. Fundforeducationabroad.org. https://fundforeducationabroad.org/journal/my-guide-to-copenhagens-public-transportation/

Copenhagen one of the best sports cities in the world. (2016, December 13). Wonderful Copenhagen. https://www.wonderfulcopenhagen.com/convention-bureau/news-room/copenhagen-one-best-sports-cities-world

Dandy. (2018, August 24). An introduction to my bit on the side – Brønshøj BK. The Dandy Dons. https://thedandydons.com/an-introduction-to-my-bit-on-the-side-bronshoj-bk/

Eiselt , D. (2024, March 22). Nørrebro, Copenhagen – all you need to know. Www.cestee.com. https://www.cestee.com/destination/denmark/copenhagen/norrebro

Explore Copenhagen off the beaten track: our guide to the best neighborhoods! (2024, March 14). Www.aprileleven.fr. https://www.aprileleven.fr/en/blog/175_discover-authentic-copenhagen-explore-little-known-neighborhoods-and-enjoy-a-local-experience.html

Family fun in Østerbro, Copenhagen. (n.d.). My Guide Copenhagen. https://www.myguidecopenhagen.com/things-to-do/family-fun/osterbro

Family fun with little ones | Copenhagen Visitor Service. (n.d.). Visitorservice.kk.dk. https://visitorservice.kk.dk/en/explore-copenhagen/navigation-amager/pa-tur-med-de-sma-i-familien

Food And Drinks about Osterbro Trips. (n.d.). Culture Trip. https://theculturetrip.com/scandinavia/denmark/copenhagen/osterbro/collections/food-and-drinks

Freija. (2018, May 10). Exploring Vesterbro, Nørrebro & Frederiksberg. Wanderlust on the Rocks. https://www.wanderlustontherocks.com/travel/hotspots/exploring-vesterbro-norrebro-frederiksberg/

God, V. (2023, May 1). AMAGER – a hidden gem in Copenhagen. Scan Magazine. https://scanmagazine.co.uk/amager-a-hidden-gem-in-copenhagen/

Great Places to Go Near Bispebjerg Cemetary in June (Updated 2024) | Trip.com Travel Guides. (n.d.). TRIP.COM. https://www.trip.com/blog/attraction/near/bispebjerg-cemetary-56820668/

Guide to hotels & accommodation in Copenhagen. (n.d.). VisitCopenhagen. https://www.visitcopenhagen.com/hotels-copenhagen

GUIDE TO THE CULTURE AND LEISURE LIFE IN COPENHAGEN. (n.d.). https://international.kk.dk/sites/default/files/2021-11/Guide%20to%20the%20culture%20and%20leisure%20life%20in%20Copenhagen.pdf

Hall, L., & Bills, J. (2024, April 5). The best restaurants in Copenhagen right now. Time out Copenhagen. https://www.timeout.com/copenhagen/restaurants/best-restaurants-in-copenhagen

Harrison, M. (2013, August 15). Lost in...Brønshøj. Lost Boyos. https://lostboyos.wordpress.com/2013/08/15/lost-in-bronshoj/

Helsingør travel. (2023, June 6). Lonely Planet. https://www.lonelyplanet.com/denmark/zealand/helsingor-elsinore

Helsingør. (2023, October 24). The Hidden North. https://thehiddennorth.com/destination/helsingor/

Hotels in Brønshøj-Husum, Copenhagen – Find cheap Brønshøj-Husum hotel deals with momondo. (n.d.). Momondo. https://www.momondo.com/hotels/copenhagen-bronshoj-husum.ksp

How to get around Denmark with public transport. (n.d.). VisitDenmark. https://www.visitdenmark.com/denmark/plan-your-trip/public-transport

How to properly do Nørrebro, the world's coolest neighbourhood. (2024, May 22). Time out Copenhagen. https://www.timeout.com/copenhagen/things-to-do/norrebro-copenhagen-neighbourhood-guide

Jacky. (2018, June 25). Ultimate Guide to Copenhagen Airport (By an Ex-Employee). Nomad Epicureans. https://www.nomadepicureans.com/europe/denmark/copenhagen-airport-guide/

Journalist, G. M. (2023, July 19). Exploring Copenhagen's Most Vibrant Neighborhood: A Day Unplanned in Nørrebro. Grady Newsource. https://gradynewsource.uga.edu/exploring-copenhagens-most-vibrant-neighborhood-a-day-unplanned-in-norrebro/

Lena. (2018, May 28). Interactive Way to Explore Nørrebro, Copenhagen. Travel Monkey. https://www.travel-monkey.com/norrebro-copenhagen/

Louisiana Museum of Modern Art, 30 minutes from Copenhagen. (2024). VisitNordsjælland. https://www.visitnorthzealand.com/north-sealand/events/louisiana-museum-modern-art-world-class-art-sea-gdk621156

Metro – Getting to & from Copenhagen Airport by Metro | CPH. (n.d.). Www.cph.dk. https://www.cph.dk/en/parking-transport/bus-train-metro-taxi/metro

Navigating Copenhagen's Neighborhoods: From Trendy Vesterbro to Charming Frederiksberg. (n.d.). Excurzilla.com. https://excurzilla.com/blog/en/denmark/navigating-copenhagens-neighborhoods-from-trendy-vesterbro-to-charming-frederiksberg

Neighborhood Guide: Amager, Denmark. (2021, September 9). DISCOVER STUDY ABROAD. https://discoverstudyabroad.org/neighborhood-guide-amager-denmark/

Niedenghraus , A. (2020, December 3). Copenhagen Airport Guide. TripSavvy. https://www.tripsavvy.com/copenhagen-airport-guide-5089927

Nørrebro. (n.d.). VisitDenmark. https://www.visitdenmark.com/denmark/plan-your-trip/norrebro-gdk957596

Østerbro Neighbourhood Guide. (n.d.). LifeX. https://www.joinlifex.com/blog/osterbro-neighbourhood-guide

Planet, L. (n.d.). Must-see attractions Nørrebro & Østerbro, Copenhagen. Lonely Planet. https://www.lonelyplanet.com/denmark/copenhagen/norre-bro-osterbro/attractions

Planet, L. (n.d.). Must-see attractions Vesterbro & Frederiksberg, Copenhagen. Lonely Planet. https://www.lonelyplanet.com/denmark/copenhagen/vesterbro-frederiksberg/attractions

Preethi. (2018, September 26). Three Days in Copenhagen (with Kids!). Local Passport Family. https://www.localpassportfamily.com/2018/09/three-days-in-copenhagen-with-kids.html

Rental unit in Frederiksberg 5.0 · 2 bedrooms · 4 beds · 1 bath. (n.d.). Airbnb. https://www.airbnb.com/rooms/48575923

Rose . (2023, September 23). 20 fun and unique things to do in Copenhagen. Getyourguide.com. https://www.getyourguide.com/explorer/copenha-gen-ttd12/fun-things-to-do-in-copenhagen/

Roskilde Festival. (2024). Roskilde-Festival.dk. https://roskilde-festival.dk/

Roskilde: Vikings, History & Heritage. (2024). Visit Copenhagen. https://www.visitcopenhagen.com/beyond-copenhagen/beyond-copenhagen/roskil-de-vikings-history-heritage

Sport and Activities | VisitCopenhagen. (n.d.). Www.visitcopenhagen.com. https://www.visitcopenhagen.com/explore/activities-cid36/sport-and-activi-ties-cid37

The 156 Best Things to Do in Amager Fælled – Booking.com. (n.d.). Www.booking.com. https://www.booking.com/attractions/city/dk/amager-faelled.en-gb.html

THE BEST 10 Restaurants near BRØNSHØJ-HUSUM, COPENHAGEN, DEN-MARK – Last Updated July 2024. (n.d.). Yelp. https://m.yelp.com/search?c-flt=restaurants&find_loc=Bronshoj

Things to Do in Bronshoj in 2024 – Top Attractions, Local Food, Hotels & Travel Tips. (n.d.). TRIP.COM. https://www.trip.com/travel-guide/destination/bronshoj-10369/

to, C. (2005, April 20). district of Copenhagen. Wikivoyage.org; Wikimedia Foundation, Inc. https://en.wikivoyage.org/wiki/Copenhagen/N%C3%B8rre-bro

Top Things To Do In Inner Osterbro . (n.d.). https://www.tripadvisor.com/At-tractions-g189541-Activities-zfn8623679-Copenhagen_Zealand.html

Unique experiences in Copenhagen | Tivoli Hotel & Congress Center. (n.d.). Tivoli Hotel & Congress Center. https://www.tivolihotel.com/experience-co-penhagen

Vladimirova, R. (2021, April 14). A Guide to Copenhagen Neighbourhoods: Østerbro. Nordgreen Global. https://nordgreen.com/blogs/nordic-culture/osterbro

What to see and do in Frederiksberg. (n.d.). VisitCopenhagen. https://www.visitcopenhagen.com/copenhagen/neighbourhoods/what-see-and-do-frederiksberg

What to see and do in Østerbro. (n.d.). VisitCopenhagen. https://www.visit-copenhagen.com/copenhagen/neighbourhoods/what-see-and-do-osterbro

What to see and do on Amager. (n.d.). VisitCopenhagen. https://www.visitco-penhagen.com/copenhagen/neighbourhoods/what-see-and-do-amager

Whyte, D. (2017, December 21). A hipster's guide to uber-cool Nørrebro. In-trepid Travel Blog. https://www.intrepidtravel.com/adventures/guide-to-nor-rebro/

IMAGE SOURCES

1   Lavantos, CC BY-SA 4.0 <https://creativecommons.org/licenses/by-sa/4.0>, via Wikimedia Commons https://commons.wikimedia.org/wiki/File:Reiterstandbild_des_Absalon_von_Lund.jpg

2   Håkan Dahlström, CC BY 2.0 <https://creativecommons.org/licenses/by/2.0>, via Wikimedia Commons https://commons.wikimedia.org/wiki/File:%C3%96resund_bridge.jpg

3   cyclonebill from Copenhagen, Denmark, CC BY-SA 2.0 <https://creativecommons.org/licenses/by-sa/2.0>, via Wikimedia Commons https://commons.wikimedia.org/wiki/File:Sm%C3%B8rrebr%C3%B8d_med_tatar_og_h%C3%B8nsesalat_(5485563164).jpg

4   Georges Biard, CC BY-SA 3.0 <https://creativecommons.org/licenses/by-sa/3.0>, via Wikimedia Commons https://commons.wikimedia.org/wiki/File:Lars_Von_Trier_Cannes_2011.jpg

5   Jules Verne Times Two / www.julesvernex2.com, CC BY-SA 4.0 <https://creativecommons.org/licenses/by-sa/4.0>, via Wikimedia Commons https://commons.wikimedia.org/wiki/File:Sunset_by_the_canal_with_the_Inderhavnsbroen_bridge_in_the_background,_Indre_By,_Copenhagen,_Denmark_(PPL1-Corrected)_julesvernex2.jpg

6   Elgaard, CC BY-SA 3.0 <http://creativecommons.org/licenses/by-sa/3.0/>, via Wikimedia Commons https://commons.wikimedia.org/wiki/File:Rosenborg_cph.jpg

7   Jay Galvin, Attribution 2.0 Generic, CC BY 2.0 <https://creativecommons.org/licenses/by/2.0/> https://www.flickr.com/photos/jaygalvin/37824339905

8   Leif Jørgensen, CC BY-SA 4.0 <https://creativecommons.org/licenses/by-sa/4.0>, via Wikimedia Commons https://commons.wikimedia.org/wiki/File:S-train_line_Bx_at_Nordhavn_Station_02.jpg

9   Mustang Joe, https://www.flickr.com/photos/mustangjoe/7625253038

10 Manfred Werner (Tsui), CC BY-SA 4.0 <https://creativecommons.org/licenses/by-sa/4.0>, via Wikimedia Commons https://commons.wikimedia.org/wiki/File:K%C3%B8benhavn_2019_08_04_f_Frederiksgade_Marmorkirken_(Frederiks_Kirke).jpg

11   Richard Mortel, Attribution 2.0 Generic, CC BY 2.0 <https://creativecommons.
      org/licenses/by/2.0/> https://www.flickr.com/photos/prof_richard/35596235203

12   Mahlum, CC BY-SA 4.0 <https://creativecommons.org/licenses/by-sa/4.0>, via
      Wikimedia Commons https://commons.wikimedia.org/wiki/File:Hirschsprungske_
      Samling_cropped.jpg

13   Alex-David Baldi, Attribution-NonCommercial-ShareAlike 2.0 Generic, <https://
      creativecommons.org/licenses/by-nc-sa/2.0/> https://www.flickr.com/photos/
      alex-david/50052044681

14   Aram Zucker-Scharff from Fairfax, VA, USA, CC BY 2.0 <https://
      creativecommons.org/licenses/by/2.0>, via Wikimedia Commons https://
      commons.wikimedia.org/wiki/File:Str%C3%B8get,_Copenhagen,_Denmark_
      (9283134442).jpg

15   Jim Nix, Attribution-NonCommercial-ShareAlike 2.0 Generic, CC BY-NC-SA 2.0
      <https://creativecommons.org/licenses/by-nc-sa/2.0/> https://www.flickr.com/
      photos/jimnix/6965276294

16   Andrzej Otrębski, CC BY-SA 4.0 <https://creativecommons.org/licenses/
      by-sa/4.0>, via Wikimedia Commons https://commons.wikimedia.org/wiki/
      File:K%C3%B8benhavn_Teatr_Kr%C3%B3lewski.jpg

17   Jakub Hałun, CC BY-SA 4.0 <https://creativecommons.org/licenses/by-
      sa/4.0>, via Wikimedia Commons https://commons.wikimedia.org/wiki/
      File:Frederiksberg_Palace_in_Frederiksberg,_Denmark,_20220617_1634_6934.jpg

18   Jonas Smith, Attribution-NonCommercial 2.0 Generic, CC BY-NC 2.0 <https://
      creativecommons.org/licenses/by-nc/2.0/> https://www.flickr.com/photos/
      jonassmith/8960324833/

19   Daniel, Attribution 2.0 Generic, CC BY 2.0 <https://creativecommons.org/
      licenses/by/2.0/> https://www.flickr.com/photos/57511216@N04/14468642681

20   Johan Jönsson (Julle), CC BY-SA 4.0 <https://creativecommons.org/licenses/
      by-sa/4.0>, via Wikimedia Commons https://commons.wikimedia.org/wiki/
      File:K%C3%B6ttbyn.jpg

21   Leif Jørgensen, CC BY-SA 4.0 <https://creativecommons.org/licenses/by-sa/4.0>,
      via Wikimedia Commons https://commons.wikimedia.org/wiki/File:Copenhagen_
      Metro_bus_line_111M_on_Istedgade_02.jpg

22   *Henrik Pedersen, Attribution-NonCommercial-ShareAlike 2.0 Generic, CC BY-NC-SA 2.0 <https://creativecommons.org/licenses/by-nc-sa/2.0/> https://www.flickr.com/photos/henrikpedersen33/35722488871*

23   *Loozrboy, Attribution-ShareAlike 2.0 Generic, CC BY-SA 2.0, <https://creativecommons.org/licenses/by-sa/2.0/> https://www.flickr.com/photos/loozrboy/5101042048/*

24   *A.Currell, Attribution-NonCommercial 2.0 Generic, CC BY-NC 2.0, <https://creativecommons.org/licenses/by-nc/2.0/> https://www.flickr.com/photos/23748404@N00/5871062117*

25   *Ramblersen2, CC BY-SA 4.0 <https://creativecommons.org/licenses/by-sa/4.0>, via Wikimedia Commons https://commons.wikimedia.org/wiki/File:S%C3%B8nder_Boulevard_03.jpg*

26   *News Oresund, CC BY 2.0 <https://creativecommons.org/licenses/by/2.0>, via Wikimedia Commons https://commons.wikimedia.org/wiki/File:Oksnehallen_Copenhagen_20130831_0327_(9640094470).jpg*

27   @markheybo from UK, CC BY 2.0 *<https://creativecommons.org/licenses/by/2.0>, via Wikimedia Commons https://commons.wikimedia.org/wiki/File:S%C3%B8erne_01.jpg*

28   *Jim Nix, Attribution-NonCommercial-ShareAlike 2.0 Generic, CC BY-NC-SA 2.0, <https://creativecommons.org/licenses/by-nc-sa/2.0/> https://www.flickr.com/photos/jimnix/7137100987*

29   *Patti Manolis, CC BY 2.0 <https://creativecommons.org/licenses/by/2.0>, via Wikimedia Commons https://commons.wikimedia.org/wiki/File:Designmuseum_Danmark.jpg*

30   *Daderot, CC0, via Wikimedia Commons https://commons.wikimedia.org/wiki/File:Stokkene,_Kastellet_-_Copenhagen_-_DSC07268.JPG*

31   *Statens Museum for Kunst, CC0, via Wikimedia Commons https://commons.wikimedia.org/wiki/File:Statens_Museum_for_Kunst,_exterior_-_Copenhagen_-_DSC08295.JPG*

32   準建築人手札網站 *Forgemind ArchiMedia from Taichung, Taiwan, Taiwan, CC BY 2.0 <https://creativecommons.org/licenses/by/2.0>, via Wikimedia Commons https://commons.wikimedia.org/wiki/File:DR_Byen_-_Segment_1.jpg*

33   *jpellgen (@1105_jp), Attribution-NonCommercial-NoDerivs 2.0 Generic, CC BY-NC-ND 2.0, <https://creativecommons.org/licenses/by-nc-nd/2.0/> https://www.flickr.com/photos/jpellgen/30689878368*

34   *Leif Jørgensen, CC BY-SA 4.0 <https://creativecommons.org/licenses/by-sa/4.0>, via Wikimedia Commons https://commons.wikimedia.org/wiki/File:Enigma_Museum_in_Copenhagen_2021.jpg*

35   *Lars K Jensen, Attribution 2.0 Generic, CC BY 2.0 <https://creativecommons.org/licenses/by/2.0/> https://www.flickr.com/photos/larskjensen/29639223587*

36   Jens Cederskjold, Attribution-ShareAlike 2.0 Generic, CC BY-SA 2.0 *<https://creativecommons.org/licenses/by-sa/2.0/> https://www.flickr.com/photos/184898381@N07/51280490229*

37   *https://www.flickr.com/photos/virtualwayfarer/14091421935/*

38   *Emily, CC BY 2.0 <https://creativecommons.org/licenses/by/2.0>, via Wikimedia Commons https://commons.wikimedia.org/wiki/File:Superkilen_hill-top_view.jpg*

39   *bynyalcin, CC BY 3.0 <https://creativecommons.org/licenses/by/3.0>, via Wikimedia Commons https://commons.wikimedia.org/wiki/File:Amager_East,_Copenhagen,_Denmark_-_panoramio.jpg*

40   *News Oresund, CC BY 2.0 <https://creativecommons.org/licenses/by/2.0>, via Wikimedia Commons https://commons.wikimedia.org/wiki/File:Den_Bla_Planet_Danmarks_akvarium_20130427_0391F_(8709639645).jpg*

41   準建築人手札網站 *Forgemind ArchiMedia from Taichung, Taiwan, Taiwan, CC BY 2.0 <https://creativecommons.org/licenses/by/2.0>, via Wikimedia Commons https://commons.wikimedia.org/wiki/File:BIG_-_8_House.jpg*

42   *Lisa Risager, Attribution-ShareAlike 2.0 Generic, CC BY-SA 2.0 <https://creativecommons.org/licenses/by-sa/2.0/> https://www.flickr.com/photos/risager/14893950872*

43   *milgrammer, CC BY 2.0 <https://creativecommons.org/licenses/by/2.0>, via Wikimedia Commons https://commons.wikimedia.org/wiki/File:Harbour_Bath,_Islands_Brygge.jpg*

44   *Thomas Vedelsbøl, CC0, via Wikimedia Commons https://commons.wikimedia.org/wiki/File:Valby_Kirke_13-07-2013.JPG*

45   *Donald Hobern from Copenhagen, Denmark, CC BY 2.0 <https://creativecommons.org/licenses/by/2.0>, via Wikimedia Commons https://commons.wikimedia.org/wiki/File:Utterslev_Mose_(38281053596).jpg*

46   *User:Nillerdk, CC BY-SA 3.0 <https://creativecommons.org/licenses/by-sa/3.0>, via Wikimedia Commons https://commons.wikimedia.org/wiki/File:Br%C3%B8nsh%C3%B8j_vandt%C3%A5rn.jpg*

47   *cjreddaway, CC BY 2.0 <https://creativecommons.org/licenses/by/2.0>, via Wikimedia Commons https://commons.wikimedia.org/wiki/File:VM_Houses.jpg*

48   *OpenStreetMap Contributors https://www.openstreetmap.org*

49   *OpenStreetMap Contributors https://www.openstreetmap.org*

50   *OpenStreetMap Contributors https://www.openstreetmap.org*

51   *OpenStreetMap Contributors https://www.openstreetmap.org*

52   *OpenStreetMap Contributors https://www.openstreetmap.org*

53   *OpenStreetMap Contributors https://www.openstreetmap.org*

54   *OpenStreetMap Contributors https://www.openstreetmap.org*

55   *OpenStreetMap Contributors https://www.openstreetmap.org*

56   *OpenStreetMap Contributors https://www.openstreetmap.org*

57   *OpenStreetMap Contributors https://www.openstreetmap.org*

58   *OpenStreetMap Contributors https://www.openstreetmap.org*

59   *OpenStreetMap Contributors https://www.openstreetmap.org*

60   *OpenStreetMap Contributors https://www.openstreetmap.org*

61   *OpenStreetMap Contributors https://www.openstreetmap.org*

62   *OpenStreetMap Contributors https://www.openstreetmap.org*

63   *OpenStreetMap Contributors https://www.openstreetmap.org*

64   *OpenStreetMap Contributors https://www.openstreetmap.org*

65 OpenStreetMap Contributors https://www.openstreetmap.org

66 OpenStreetMap Contributors https://www.openstreetmap.org

67 Nick, Attribution-NonCommercial-NoDerivs 2.0 Generic, CC BY-NC-ND 2.0 <https://creativecommons.org/licenses/by-nc-nd/2.0/ > https://www.flickr.com/photos/34517490@N00/37712220492

68 CucombreLibre from New York, NY, USA, CC BY-SA 4.0 <https://creativecommons.org/licenses/by-sa/4.0>, via Wikimedia Commons https://commons.wikimedia.org/wiki/File:Roskilde_Cathedral_aerial_crop.jpg

69 Hagai Agmon-Snir חچای اچمون-سنیر حگی اگمون-سنیر, CC BY-SA 4.0 <https://creativecommons.org/licenses/by-sa/4.0>, via Wikimedia Commons https://commons.wikimedia.org/wiki/File:KronborgCastleDenmarkOct152022_06.jpg

70 Erik Christensen, CC BY-SA 3.0 <https://creativecommons.org/licenses/by-sa/3.0>, via Wikimedia Commons https://commons.wikimedia.org/wiki/File:M%C3%B8ns_Klint.1.JPG

71 Michael, Attribution-NonCommercial-ShareAlike 2.0 Generic, CC BY-NC-SA 2.0 <https://creativecommons.org/licenses/by-nc-sa/2.0/> https://www.flickr.com/photos/mr172/5695591734